Cognitive Behavioral Therapy Workbook for Anxiety

A 7-Step Program to Overcome Your Fear, Panic, Anxiety, and Worry

Antonio Matteo Bruscella

DEDICATION

To Paola e Michele for their amazing love and support.

A.M.B.

TABLE OF CONTENTS

INTRODUCTION

Have you ever felt that gut-wrenching moment where your heart pounds against your chest and you are suddenly convinced you are in imminent danger, even when there is nothing threatening you? You may feel clammy, scared, and unable to focus on anything other than the sheer panic running through you. During an anxiety attack like this, you may feel completely paralyzed and unable to function. This anxiety can get so bad that you find yourself struggling to get through your day-to-day life, no matter how hard you try.

When anxiety has you caught in its clutches, it is easy to feel hopeless or trapped, especially if you have tried and failed to work through your problems in the past. Please know that *Cognitive Behavioral Therapy Workbook for Anxiety: A 7-Step Program to Overcome your Fear, Panic, Anxiety, and Worry* is here to hold your hand and guide you, step by step, through getting a handle on your anxious feelings. With this book, you will be walked through seven steps, designed to teach you the skills you need to learn to manage your anxiety on your own.

First, you will be taught all you need to know about fear and anxiety, as well as how they can impact your day-to-day life. You will be provided with information on cognitive behavioral therapy (CBT), an extremely effective therapy, as well as why it works. You will then be walked through how to use this book to utilize what is written to its fullest extent.

From there, you will be guided through the seven steps you will need to follow in order to complete the CBT process for anxiety. Each of these seven steps will compound on themselves, providing you with what you need to know, as well as giving you three different assignments per step that will aid you in conquering your anxiety once and for all, without ever having to consult a licensed professional.

It is important to note, however, that while this workbook is designed to provide you with information on anxiety and suggest some strategies you can utilize to manage your symptoms of anxiety and worry, it is NOT a substitute for a proper diagnosis, treatment, or the advice of an appropriate health professional. The book is a fantastic reference, but will never be able to provide you the individualized care a licensed health professional could offer. If your symptoms are severe or overwhelming, or if you have never seen a doctor about your mental health symptoms, it is important to seek advice from a qualified health professional. Likewise, this book does not advise you to alter any medication that has been prescribed, and you should always seek medical advice before altering your medication regimen. If you ever feel as if you may hurt yourself or others, please consider this a medical emergency and call your local emergency services hotline, or seek treatment in an emergency room.

Remember, no matter how severe your symptoms may seem or feel, you can fix things. If not through this book, then through seeking help from a licensed therapist or taking medication. No matter how bad your anxiety feels, or how hopeless it may seem at times, you can make things better. You deserve to live a life free from the constant tendrils of fear and anxiety. You deserve to live a life you can enjoy without worry or fear. You deserve to live a life where you do more than just survive. You can, and you will attain the life you wish to lead with perseverance and effort. No matter how hard things may get, remember to keep your goals in mind, and never stop striving for them. Happiness and mental wellness are within your reach, even if your anxiety has fooled you into thinking otherwise.

Part I

Everything You Need to Know Before Starting the CBT Workbook

CHAPTER 1: FEAR AND ANXIETY

Fear and anxiety may seem similar, but they are two different feelings. While they both involve stress responses, they are reactions to different types of threats. Anxiety is a reaction to the idea of a threat: It keeps you on edge and apprehensive, heightening your awareness so you can respond to any potential threats quickly. Fear, on the other hand, is a response to a known threat. Rather than being alert in case of a threat, you are reacting to something that is actively threatening you. This distinction is necessary to make, as fear can cause anxiety symptoms, but true anxiety does not directly cause fear. Understanding these nuances, as well as how to identify when what you are feeling is fear or anxiety, will help you learn to control your feelings of anxiety or worry. After all, anxiety is a feeling that something bad is coming, not that there is a threat present.

Symptoms of Anxiety

Anxiety attacks can take many forms. Sometimes, they present as aggression, while other times, you may feel frozen in fear. In the heart of an anxiety attack, you feel as though there is danger surrounding you, and no matter how hard you try to tell yourself that you are okay, you cannot shake the fear of imminent danger. This often manifests in any combination of the following symptoms:

- Overwhelming fear or sense of imminent death or harm
- Chest pain and heart palpitations

- Shortness of breath and choking sensation
- Trembling, numbness, and chills or hot flashes
- Nausea and dizziness
- Feeling as though you have detached from the world around you (called derealization)

All of these symptoms could be signs of anxiety, but also signs of serious medical problems. If you feel these symptoms regularly, even when there is no apparent danger around you, it is worth getting a checkup from a licensed medical professional. Your primary physician can eliminate any worry that there is a more sinister cause of your symptoms, and also refer you to a mental health expert that will be able to accurately pinpoint your diagnosis and help you on the journey toward wellness.

Healthy Fear and Anxiety

As unpleasant as both fear and anxiety are, they are both healthy and normal feelings, in moderation. They each have very specific biological purposes, and when they are functioning normally, they both work together to keep you alive. Imagine if you are faced with someone with a gun: Your gut reaction will likely be fear. This fear will start your fight-or-flight reflex, and with adrenaline coursing through your veins, you will be able to focus better on what is happening, so you can react to movements quicker. Your muscles will be ready to burst into action to either fight or run. Your endurance will increase. All of these together will prepare you to protect your life, allowing you to either flee from the person with a gun or fight off the person with the gun.

Likewise, with anxiety, your body is reacting to the idea of a threat. There may not be a threat that you are aware of, but you do feel as though there might be one somewhere nearby, and that apprehension is enough to keep you prepared to launch into fight-or-flight mode at a moment's notice. If you are walking through a dark alley at night, you may feel that anxiety gnawing at you, telling you to stay on edge and alert for any threats that may potentially jump out at you. That anxiety warns you that there may be a danger, and in healthy individuals, this anxiety is balanced. It will keep you alert when your surroundings dictate that you probably should be, such as when you walk through a dark alley, or when you are hiking through a mountain trail at dusk: Your alertness keeps you prepared to react to any sort of threat that may arise. For people without anxiety disorders, it is smart to pay attention to these gut feelings, as we often have them for good reasons, such as knowing that we are in a dangerous area or that we are doing something risky.

When Fear and Anxiety Become Problematic

For someone with an anxiety disorder, however, they frequently feel that state of constant alertness and worry even when it is unwarranted, leaving them unable to relax and constantly hyper-aware of their surroundings. These symptoms can begin to spill into other aspects of your life, and when they become a persistent problem, repeatedly impeding on your ability to function or enjoy day-to-day life, your anxiety may be problematic. Only you, yourself, can identify when your anxiety has become a problem. In order to do so, you can ask yourself a few questions. Is your anxiety unwarranted? Is it persistent, no matter how irrational you may think it is? Is there a recurring cause to it? Is it becoming so bad that you have to rearrange your life to accommodate your negative feelings? Is it becoming so bad that your friends and family have begun to mention or question your anxiety? When your anxiety is triggered, are you unable to react in a rational or healthy way? Do you feel as though you cannot cope with your anxiety at this moment? Is your anxiety becoming overwhelming?

These questions can help you gauge your own opinions or feelings about your anxiety. If you can answer yes to any of them, you may have a problem with anxiety, and speaking to a medical professional would likely be beneficial to you. The professionals are trained to walk you through the steps of healing and to control your anxiety, so please do not feel intimidated or afraid of seeking help. If your anxiety is truly problematic, you will likely need some intervention, whether through self-help books such as this one or through working with a therapist, to begin coping in a healthy, efficient manner.

Common Anxiety Disorders

Anxiety on its own does not refer to one specific problem. It is a spectrum of disorders that can come in a wide range of shapes and forms, some of which seem to be intuitively related to anxiety, while others may not seem obviously related. Ultimately, each of the following disorders you will read about is related to anxiety, though each present in different ways. All of them relate to stress or anxiety responses for a variety of reasons. Here is a general overview of the most common anxiety disorders.

Generalized Anxiety Disorder (GAD)

GAD is characterized primarily by chronic feelings of anxiety, even when unprovoked. The sufferer often feels a persistent, extreme sense of worry or fear, as well as the symptoms listed above. In order to be persistent, the feelings of anxiety must be present for the majority of days for at least half a year. They are general, meaning there is no particular trigger, and the symptoms of anxiety are felt in a wide range of circumstances, such as work, driving, or even social interactions with friends or family. Oftentimes, they are pervasive, meaning they are significantly impacting the sufferer's life in a negative fashion. For example, if the sufferer feels anxiety when forced to present for class, she may fail multiple assignments that involve public speaking. Likewise, a person who is anxious when talking to strangers may intentionally avoid all unnecessary contact with other people, costing him his social life. Since the anxiety occurs in a wide range of situations, it may lead to the sufferer attempting to avoid everything possible in hopes of avoiding the feelings of anxiety they fear, which really only exacerbates the situation. When fearing anxiety itself, the sufferer may find him or herself becoming anxious at the thought of becoming anxious.

Panic Disorder

Panic disorder is typically described as unexpected episodes of intense, overwhelming terror along with the physical symptoms typically experienced with anxiety in the absence of any true danger. This must happen more than once, and the sufferer will often feel an overwhelming sense of losing control and a sense of impending demise. There is no known cause for these panic attacks, though it is believed that genetics, stress, and a sensitive temperament can leave an individual at a higher risk for suffering from these debilitating symptoms. Without seeking treatment, panic disorder can impact most aspects of daily life. The fear of another panic attack can cause you to develop phobias, feel as though you must seek medical treatment for other issues that may not even be present, cause issues with work and school, increase the occurrence of suicidal thoughts, and risk of substance abuse and addiction.

Obsessive-Compulsive Disorder (OCD)

OCD, as the name implies, involves a series of obsessions and compulsions. Obsessions are thoughts that repeatedly occur, even why you try to stop or resist them and are typically disturbing in some way, shape, or form. Even if the person suffering from OCD is aware that the obsessions are irrational, they cannot be stopped. They are time-consuming and inhibit the individual's ability to function normally.

Compulsions are repetitive behaviors or thoughts that are acted upon with the intention of stopping the obsessions. The person with OCD recognizes that the relief from the obsession will only occur temporarily and that it may be irrational, but cannot help him or herself. This coping mechanism is frequently time-consuming, and the repetitiveness of the compulsions detract from day-to-day life. Compulsions are context-dependent, meaning that for some, a specific action might be compulsion when it is entirely normal, or even expected for others. For example, someone who works in a kitchen may wash his or her hand's hundreds of times throughout the day due to touching different substances whereas someone with an obsession over cleanliness might compulsively wash his or her hand's hundreds of times for no real reason other than to get rid of the obsessive thoughts. Clearly, the person working in a restaurant needs to keep hands clean and will be handling multiple products that will call for hands to be clean, but a person sitting at home has no reason to wash his or her hands so often.

Phobias

Phobias are intense fears or aversion to specific stimuli. For example, one of the most common phobias is toward spiders. Someone with a spider phobia may have irrational reactions to seeing or even thinking about possibly seeing a spider, and will likely intentionally change how things are done or where he or she goes to avoid spiders. If a spider is encountered, people with arachnophobia typically experience intense anxiety. Phobias can be specific or general, and range from fearing a specific animal or insect to fearing a concept, or even fearing specific shapes and smells. There is even a phobia specific to tiny holes on a background, such as the pitting of strawberry seeds on fruit, called trypophobia. These phobias can be somewhat innocuous, such as fearing spiders, but also completely overwhelming and detrimental to day-to-day life, such as fearing to drive, fly, or even leave the house.

Social Anxiety Disorder

Social anxiety disorder is quite similar to a phobia and used to be referred to as social phobia instead of social anxiety disorder. People with this form of anxiety feel an intense fear toward being judged or rejected in social situations. Oftentimes, they fear that their behaviors rooted in anxiety, such as blushing or stuttering, will be seen negatively by others, and because of this, they avoid social interactions as much as possible. When they have no option to avoid being in a social setting, they often experience intense physical symptoms of anxiety, ranging from heart palpitations, nausea, and sometimes, even full panic attacks. This can be a general fear of social interactions in general or be related to specific contexts, such as at work, or in school. Despite that, they are oftentimes aware of how irrational, excessive, and unrealistic their fears are, they feel powerless to stop the feelings. This can cause significant issues in one's day-to-day life, such as inhibiting the ability to work or avoiding social events with friends, causing their relationships to fail.

Post-Traumatic Stress Disorder (PTSD)

PTSD occurs after a trauma, which is typically some form of violence that was suffered but can also include accidents, natural disasters, being diagnosed with a terminal or life-threatening illness, or any other event that the sufferer has deemed traumatic. This anxiety disorder is typically characterized by intense anxiety symptoms related to a specific traumatic event and lasting at least one month. Typically, the onset of symptoms begins within three months of the event, but can sometimes happen later.

This disorder involves being fine one moment, but then suddenly being stuck in flashbacks of the event, leading to anxiety symptoms. In order to warrant a diagnosis of PTSD, there must be six criteria identified:

- Experiencing some sort of trauma that involves a response of helplessness and fear
- Reliving the event (flashbacks)
- Avoiding things related to the event that may be triggers
- Issues with sleep and concentration. Increased vigilance with exaggerated startle responses
- Long-lasting (at least one month)
- Day-to-day functioning has been impaired

CHAPTER 2: UNDERSTANDING COGNITIVE BEHAVIORAL THERAPY

Experiencing a wide range of emotions, both positive and negative, is a normal part of being human. Even negative emotions can be healthy, while others are unhealthy, and when your emotions are becoming unhealthy, leading to negative behaviors that begin to influence the rest of your life, you may decide that you need to make a change somehow. Cognitive behavioral therapy is a frequently used therapy that enables changes in behaviors.

What is CBT?

As the name implies, CBT is a therapy involving cognitions, or thoughts, and behaviors. This form of psychotherapy (also known as talk therapy) is largely effective at enabling people to make substantial behavioral changes. This is done by recognizing the cycle between thoughts, feelings, and behaviors. Thoughts will influence how you feel, and how you feel dictates how you behave. CBT aims to take the best of cognitive therapy with behavior therapy, creating an entirely new hybrid that focuses on that cycle.

Specifically, CBT will teach you how to disrupt the cycle by identifying the cause of your behaviors and teaching you how to correct them. For example, if you know that the thought of driving will trigger an anxiety attack, CBT will work with you to slowly change your thoughts and feelings that surround the idea of driving until your thoughts become healthier and more productive, enabling you to drive without the anxiety attack. By changing your thoughts on driving, when you are faced with having to drive, you will no longer feel anxious because your thoughts have changed. Because you no longer feel anxious, you will be able to drive.

CBT Key Principles

There are four key principles that enable CBT to be as effective as it is. These four principles aid the therapist in creating long-term changes to your behaviors in a brief time frame. Utilizing these principles, CBT has developed such a good reputation that even the United States military touts its success and utilizes it to help a wide range of patients due to the effectiveness and relatively quick turnaround CBT employs.

Goal-oriented

CBT is goal-oriented, meaning it heavily employs goals Due to its nature as problem-solving therapy, it makes sense that CBT would focus heavily on employing goals; after all, solving a problem is easier when goals are set. When you have a goal of fixing a certain problematic behavior, CBT becomes more efficient in that it can provide you with tools to fix said problematic behavior. This enables you to solve your own problem without the therapist solving it for you. These goals can be anything from solving problems to creating new healthy habits, and CBT will help you attain it. In fact, setting goals will be the focus of Part II Step 1: Setting Goals. Please see that section for further information about CBT's use of goals.

Present-focused

Along with setting goals, CBT focuses on the present. This means that CBT is more concerned with identifying and fixing current triggers as opposed to identifying what the original trigger was. For example, if, due to being abandoned by a parent as a young child, you have issues with relationships now, CBT will focus on your current triggers as opposed to the cause of them. By focusing on the present with the intention of changing your reactions to specific triggers, you take another step closer to achieving your goals. Also, with the methods CBT employs, you learn the skills to create a nearly permanent fix to your problem.

The past is important and should not be disregarded, but it does not necessarily provide the kind of insight that will be necessary to fix the problematic behaviors.

Ultimately, the past can never be changed, which is why CBT puts more emphasis on the present, but you can change your current feelings on the past, which will also lead to changes in behaviors.

Active

CBT focuses on being active, meaning that the patient will actively be making changes to his or her life and behavior as opposed to passively discussing traumas in order to try to bring about acceptance.

CBT will teach multiple strategies, skills, and techniques that will help you learn how to cope with a wide range of problems. It will also require you to engage in the active practice of your skills in real life though homework assignments assigned by a therapist if you are seeing one, or by yourself if you are attempting the CBT process on your own.

By actively practicing these skills, you will solidify their use as a habit that you will fall back on when needed as opposed to relying on any coping mechanisms that you may have developed that are unhealthy or unproductive.

Brief

CBT is brief: It on average lasts a dozen sessions, give or take a few before you are set out into the world on your own. Many other forms of psychotherapy, on the other hand, may take years of regular sessions before you feel confident enough to end your appointments, and your therapist will walk you through a wide range of problems, one at a time. In contrast, CBT focuses on teaching you the skills first so you can apply them on your own. It seeks to make you self-sufficient sooner, and with the skills you learn, you will feel less need to seek a therapist to help you work through the problems that you can solve yourself.

CBT Key Concepts

Along with those key principles, CBT consists of a few key concepts. Consider this section your glossary for the most common terms you will come across during the course of reading this book. Before you begin the process of trying to fix your anxiety with CBT, you must have a basic understanding of the fundamentals. These are the concepts that will be essential to this book, though there are others within CBT

Automatic Thoughts

Automatic thoughts are snap judgments, thoughts that happen on their own without your input. They are thoughts that underlie your actions and feelings that your mind does not deem important enough to be part of your conscious thoughts. They arise and are quickly forgotten or disregarded, as there is little relevance to your day. While typing, you do not think about every individual finger's movements as they happen, as that would take up far too much of your valuable mental real estate. Instead, those automatic thoughts control your hands, and as you think the words you want to type, your hands follow. The typing is reactionary to your automatic thoughts.

While automatic thoughts can free up much of your mental energy for more important tasks, they can also be negative. These thoughts can be quite insidious, as you do not pay them any attention, even when they are coloring your behaviors. At this point, automatic thoughts are referred to as negative automatic thoughts. CBT frequently aims to correct such negative automatic thoughts through various methods. These thoughts will convince you that you are worthless, useless, powerless, unloved, or any other negative feelings that may arise. For example, if you make a mistake during an interview for a new job, you may immediately get angry, telling yourself that of course, you failed the interview; you are useless and stupid, and this proves it. Your underlying negative automatic thoughts convince you to beat yourself up over a simple mistake.

Cognitive Distortions

Cognitive distortions are types of automatic thoughts, but these ones are not only negative; they are also inaccurate or distorted. These are beliefs that you may have come to accept, but in reality, they are inaccurate. These are frequently ideas such as believing that your spouse is angry with you because he or she took ten minutes to respond to your text message earlier in the day. In reality, your spouse was probably only busy, but cognitive distortions convince you otherwise. You may justify this with other negative thoughts, such as you always annoy your spouse, which likely is untrue on its own.

Cognitive distortions take a variety of forms, and being able to identify them can be particularly tricky without practice and assistance. They typically follow very specific patterns, which will be their defining features when determining whether some of your core beliefs or automatic thoughts are distorted. This will be further discussed in Part II Step 5: Identifying Negative Thinking and Cognitive Distortions.

Cognitive Restructuring

Cognitive restructuring is the process of changing how you think is called. In CBT, you will learn to recognize the relationship between thoughts, feelings, and behaviors, and you will learn about how cyclical the three are. In CBT, you seek to interrupt that cycle somehow to change the whole thing. If you can change a single part of the cycle, usually, the other two parts will automatically change as well. For example, if the thought of spiders falling on you makes you feel anxious, which in turn makes you avoid any sort of outdoors activities, you would seek to disrupt the cycle somewhere. The easiest would be to remove the thoughts of negativity around spiders. If you learn to alter your thoughts about spiders, instead of recognizing that they are not harmful to you and the likelihood of one falling on you from a tree is pretty low, you can eliminate your feelings of anxiety. With the anxiety lifted, you then feel like going into nature is not as daunting. Now, this example is obviously simplified to make it easier to understand, but the process is largely the same, no matter what the thought-feeling-behavior cycle you seek to disrupt is.

Core Beliefs

Everyone has deep-seated beliefs about him or herself. They may be positive or negative, but regardless of what they are, they will color your perceptions of the world and your behaviors. While these core beliefs are unconscious, you can identify them through introspection. You will develop these core beliefs during childhood. These beliefs are typically rigid, and you may even try to force what is happening around you to fit into the paradigms of your core beliefs, disregarding the parts that contradict the narrative you have created.

For example, if you, with your anxiety, believe that you are less deserving of respect and compassion, you may inherently act as if you are not allowed to make mistakes. When you do make one, you may be unnecessarily harsh on yourself, even when you would have treated someone else who had made that same mistake with the compassion you deserved. This belief that you are less deserving of compassion causes you to beat yourself up over simple mistakes, and if you are not in tune with your deepest core beliefs, you are not likely to notice those feelings of worthlessness underlying every time you begin to talk down to yourself.

Emotional Triggers

Sometimes, people feel intense emotion for no particularly rational reason. You could have been happily talking to someone when suddenly, you find yourself deep in a panic attack and feeling as though you are drowning with no way out. This is called being emotionally triggered, and it can happen when you least expect it for reasons you may not expect. Your reaction can range from fear to anger to intense sadness. Any emotion here is valid.

Typically, emotional triggers are related to the trauma of some sort. The trauma leaves marks on you that leave you reacting strongly to things that resemble or remind you of the traumatic event. For example, someone who was abused may be triggered by hearing something his or her abuser would frequently say, or someone with PTSD from war may be triggered by cars backfiring. Learning to understand what emotional triggers are is the first step toward learning how to correct them.

CHAPTER 3: WHY CBT WORKS

CBT has been shown to be effective in alleviating symptoms in a wide range of mental health issues, ranging from addiction to schizophrenia, along with almost everything in between. It has been shown to be effective for longer than medication and other forms of therapies. Since CBT focuses so much on providing coping skills, people who have completed this form of therapy find themselves more prepared to handle any situation life can throw at them, causing a more permanent alleviation of unmanageable symptoms. Even medication, which absolutely can be effective at alleviating symptoms, and maybe a crucial part of your plan for mental wellness, does not have as long-lasting effects as CBT. If medication is ever discontinued, symptoms often relapse shortly after.

CBT is so effective for one major reason: It returns control back to you. So many of the anxiety symptoms felt revolve around a lack of perceived control over the situation, and through CBT and learning the skills you need to cope, you are given the control of the situation. A lot of the lack of control stems from the emotional part of your brain overriding the logical part. When the emotional part is louder, you feel as though you have to pay attention. However, when you learn to focus on the logical part of your mind, those feelings of emotional turmoil and powerlessness begin to fade away. Remember, emotions are irrational; they are swayed by everything from the color of the shirt you are wearing to how bad traffic was that morning. By letting emotions rule your life, you will struggle to find the stability your life needs for you to feel in control.

When you are given the knowledge of how your thoughts work, you will learn just how profoundly one single negative thought can ripple throughout other aspects. Each negative thought you learn to create causes a domino effect, causing more and more positive, healthy thoughts, which, in turn, create positive, healthy behaviors. Those healthy behaviors encourage more healthy thoughts, and soon, you found aspects of your life that you thought were entirely unrelated are improving as well.

CBT, despite the fact that it is shorter than most other types of therapy, teaches a multitude of skills and coping mechanisms to give you all of the tools you will need. Empowered by the knowledge and skills CBT provides you, you are able to make yourself self-sufficient. By learning to cope on your own, you eliminate the majority of the need to go to therapy, which is intended to help you cope. You may even eliminate the need for medication in some instances when medication is used to mitigate symptoms as opposed to treating underlying chemical imbalances. Oftentimes, with anxiety disorders, medication is used to relax or sedate the user in order to alleviate the symptoms of anxiety. However, these medications can be addictive, and also can be so debilitating that the sufferer cannot go about day-to-day functions while taking them. With CBT, you will learn coping skills to try to mitigate the need for medication altogether, as when the anxiety gets bad, you will have the skills you need to combat it.

Remember, you should not mess with your prescribed medication regimen without first discussing it with the doctor that prescribed it, as ultimately, he or she will be able to guide you through the steps of weaning off of your medication, and will be able to judge your situation to determine whether your medication is necessary. Ultimately, if medication is a necessary tool for you, you should continue it, as the most important part of this process is ensuring that you are happy and mentally healthy. You deserve to be comfortable in your mind without worrying about anxiety symptoms preventing you from functioning, and identifying the method that will work for you is a trial and error process. CBT, while effective for many people, will not work for everyone, and that should be considered.

Further, CBT works because it causes real changes in your life. When you engage in CBT with a therapist, you will be given homework assignments regularly to get you practicing the methods provided to you and to get you used to implement these changes in real time. Think of CBT as a crash course in learning coping mechanisms, and the only real way to learn them is to engage in plenty of practice. In CBT sessions, your therapist will teach you new methods, practice them with you, and then send you out to add them to your life. At your next session, you would then have a short review session in which you would reflect on the impact these coping mechanisms had on your life, and your therapist would provide insight or advice on how to change things further to work for you. However, if you are not yet interested or able to see a therapist, you will have to create these assignments and goals for yourself.

This book will provide you with sample assignments for each and every step of the CBT process, but you will have to actively tweak them to fit your situation. You will have to remain engaged and motivated to continue the process on your own without a therapist holding you accountable. The structured nature of CBT works to hold you accountable and is one of the key components of the therapy as a whole. The only way you can mimic this is by forcing yourself to stick to a realistic schedule that you set up for yourself when you begin. Of course, one of the biggest benefits of attempting the CBT process on your own is the ability to be flexible, but remember that you should be regularly working on your mental health, and setting schedules and set times for when your complete parts are necessary.

Remember to try to preserve the key components of CBT for maximum effectiveness, and recognize that one of the primary reasons CBT is so effective is due to those components. By honoring those, you will see the fullest benefits CBT has to offer.

CHAPTER 4: HOW TO BE SUCCESSFUL USING THIS BOOK

As briefly mentioned in the previous section, CBT is primarily completed through sessions with a therapist. However, this book is seeking to teach you the skills a therapist would without needing to go to expensive sessions. Again, remember that this book is not, and does not aim to be, a substitute for a licensed medical professional, and if you feel that your symptoms are too bad to cope with on your own, seeking professional help is in your best interest.

In order to get the most out of this book, remember the four key components of CBT. It is goal-oriented, present-focused, brief, and structured. It helps to honor these four components to create the truest form of individual CBT as you can manage. You should seek to create good, structured goals, which will be the first step in the CBT process. It helps when you set up a schedule of events, perhaps choosing to do one step of the seven in a week's period, with plenty of time set for completing each step and beginning to implement them into your life. For example, maybe you read the chapter on Monday and identify what the goal of the week is. Week one, for example, is to set goals. You should read over the chapter and ensure that you have a good understanding of what makes well-formed goals entails. From there, you should complete activity 1, which would be identifying and creating goals. Week one also involves creating a calendar toward completing your goals, which should be made day three of the week. The last activity of step one is tracking progress. You should aim to track it regularly throughout the week (and through the duration of your goal). Each day during this week, you should strive to work toward the goals you have set.

The idea is that this book has multiple activities that will help you complete the steps. The activities are meant to be support for the step, and they should be completed in whatever order makes the most sense to you. If you feel like completing activity 2 would be more beneficial done first, then you have the control to do that. Ultimately, your job will be to tweak these assignments to benefit you, as you do not have the advantage of a therapist who can look over the situation and tailor each step to your specific situation.

Remember, the first part of this book is your reference center. If you ever feel as though you do not understand one of the steps in the book, it is totally okay, and even expected for you to go back to one of the prior chapters for clarification. You will need basic ideas and concepts to truly complete the CBT process in an effective manner, and with those foundations, you will find yourself successful in completing your steps and working towards restructuring your thoughts.

Keep in mind that, while you can adjust the order of the steps in the book, it is not recommended, as oftentimes, the steps build on top of each other. For example, the entire process cannot begin until you have clearly identified goals, so you know what you are aiming to achieve. Likewise, you cannot complete Step 3: Desensitizing Yourself to Triggers until you have completed Step 2: Identifying Triggers. Try to keep the order of steps in their provided form, but feel free to tweak the activities within them. By following the steps, one by one, you will eventually reach cognitive restructuring, which will help you with your symptoms of anxiety.

Remember, this process will not be easy. While it is broken up nicely in steps that may appear manageable at a glance, it involves tearing down some of your innermost thoughts and identifying why you behave the way you do. You will likely have to prove some of your deepest beliefs false, which involves a deeply personal process that can be quite painful as you go through the period of cognitive dissonance. Imagine if you were told a basic fact you have accepted is false: You would be devastated. For example, finding out that your father is not actually your father would be an earth-shattering conclusion to reach as an adult who has grown up thinking a specific person fathered you. While your cognitive distortions may not be as extreme, they will still require you to accept that you were wrong.

It is important for you to work through this process, as the most important breakthroughs during the process involve challenging your own thoughts and feelings to create the changes you desire to see. Remember, you are completing this process because you do not like the way you think, feel, or act. Changing these automatic functions requires an immense amount of effort. If you ever feel overwhelmed or as though this process is too hard for you to work through on your own, there is no shame in putting the book down and seeking a licensed therapist. Ultimately, your goal is to become healthy, and that is the most important part. With perseverance and effort, you will manage to achieve your goals. The pain and discomfort as you challenge some of your most foundational beliefs will be worth it when you achieve the mental state you desire. Remember, you can, and you will do this.

Part II

Cognitive Behavioral Therapy 7 Step Workbook and Activities

STEP 1: SETTING GOALS

Goals are great to keep you on track and to keep yourself self-motivated. They also allow you to identify problems that need to be solved. By deciding what you are striving for in life, you have a clear idea of what you are trying to accomplish with your actions. It is easier to motivate yourself to work toward a meaningful goal than it is to try to convince yourself to make changes for arbitrary reasons. For example, which sounds more compelling: Working to save money for nothing in particular, or to save money for a house in two years? Likely, having the image of the house in your mind will be significantly more motivating than just saving the money arbitrarily. You know you are working toward something you desire, and that has meaning that is motivating.

In this step of CBT, you will seek to identify your goals. Goals can be anything: You could want to learn a new instrument or to change your reaction when you feel an anxiety attack starting, to saving a certain amount of money. The point of the goals important to this process, however, involve you identifying what aspects of your mental health need help. Perhaps you have a strong phobia that is keeping you home-bound, or maybe you have PTSD symptoms after a trauma, or you have general anxiety that you would like to control. No matter what part of your mental health you would like to change, you should seek to identify it. Once you have a general idea of what you would like, it is time to start identifying how to form your goal in a way that it will be effective and beneficial on your journey.

Bad Goals

Before we begin to identify how to structure a good goal, you must first learn what to avoid. Knowing what types of goals are unproductive or difficult to attain will help you keep your own goals realistic. There are three main types of goals you should avoid setting for yourself as they do not provide you with the mindset you will need to be healthy. These types of goals are those that are emotional-based, focused on the past, or goals that are rooted in the negative somehow. All three of these are poorly formed and counterproductive for a variety of reasons.

Emotions

Focusing on feeling or not feeling certain emotions are unproductive. Oftentimes, people tell themselves, "I want to be happy again," or, "I want to feel fulfilled." The problem with this, however, is that feelings are fickle and fleeting: They are constantly changing for arbitrary reasons, and even the direction the wind blows can influence your mood, so setting a goal based on feeling a certain way.

Along with fleeting and fickle, emotions are very temporary. You will never only feel one way for an extended period of time, no matter how hard you might want to. There is no way for you to be happy all of the time, so if you set your goal of being happy, you will frequently feel as though you have not achieved said goal. Every time a negative emotion comes up, it will have the added fuel of you feeling like a failure because you obviously have not completed your goal if you are feeling upset, angry, or sad. Since emotions are so unstable, easily influenced, and unpredictable, even in the most stable of people, they should be avoided as specific goals.

Past-oriented

Another common goal that people try to set for themselves is to return to the past. Especially after going through some trauma, people often say, "I want to be happy like I used to be," or, "I want to be my old self again." The problem with these is that they look at the past. The past is something that can never be returned to, so by trying to make the old you, your new goal, you are striving for something unattainable. Your experiences will always be a part of you. You will never be who you used to be. You did not know the things you know now. Remember, CBT is present-oriented, not past-oriented, and as such, you should make sure your goals are not past-oriented.

Negative or Avoidant

Remember, the whole point of CBT is to restructure thinking, with a goal of turning your thoughts from negative to positive. When you decide to make your goal inherently negative, through using words like never or not, you are keeping your thinking in negatives. For that reason, the wording of your goal is important, and you must strive to ensure that your goals are formulated in such a way that they are positively based as opposed to negatively.

Likewise, your goals should never be based on avoiding something. Avoiding, as opposed to fixing, will leave you feeling more anxious about feeling your anxiety, which really only sends you spiraling deeper into your anxiety.

Focusing on avoiding as opposed to coping with or fixing the problem will set you up for failure, as you will feel as though you have failed every time you do encounter your negative symptoms. Constantly living in fear of feeling your symptoms that you are trying to avoid will only cause you to feel your symptoms more severely when they do arise. Instead, you should focus on goals that are active and positive.

SMART Goals

With an idea of what to avoid, you now can move on to understanding what makes a goal good. When you are trying to learn new things, acronyms are always helpful, as they give you one thing to remember to use as a prompt for all of the parts.

When thinking about goals, remember that you want to set SMART goals in order to maximize efficiency and effectiveness. SMART stands for specific, measurable, attainable, relevant, and timely. By remembering this acronym, you have the prompt necessary to create goals that are effective and achievable.

Specific

By making your goal specific, you paint a clearer picture of what you are striving to achieve. Just as when writing, you should seek out the most specific words possible in order to convey your point, you should make your goals as specific as possible. Think of saying, "An animal is coming," as opposed to, "A big, black cat is softly padding toward me." One gives you a general idea while the other paints a more specific picture. You want to paint yourself a picture of exactly what you want to achieve for your goal. If your goal is to manage anxiety, figure out how that looks specifically. Maybe, as a result of your anxiety, you have a tendency to shut down and become entirely unreceptive to everything around you, and you want to stop that. Remember, your goal should not be negative, so you must figure out how to word that in a way that is positive and specific. Perhaps you decide that your goal is to avoid shutting down. Instead of deciding upon avoiding shutting down, you can transform your goal into, "I will reduce the number of times I shut down in response to my anxiety." Now, you have a more specific goal that also recognizes that you likely will continue to have some instances of shutting down due to your anxiety, even if you are actively trying to prevent them. In this instance, having a negative response to your anxiety is not the end of the world, and does not mean that you have failed.

Measurable

Along with specific goals, you need to have a goal that is measurable in some way, shape, or form. You need to be able to see at a glance whether or not you have failed at your goal, and by assuring it is in a quantifiable form, you will be able to determine whether or not you have achieved it at a glance. Measurable can take many forms: It can be that you want to write a novel of a certain length, or save a certain amount of money, get a job with a certain salary, or even reducing your reactions to certain stimuli by a certain percentage.

With the example of controlling how often you shut down in the face of anxiety, perhaps you decide that you will reduce the number of times you react that way by 50%. You now know that you want to reduce a specific action and have a measurable, quantifiable end to your goal. You will know that you have succeeded when you are able to cut the frequency of freezing up in half.

Attainable

You should also only set goals that are attainable. This means that your goals should be something that is possible for you to reasonably complete. The easiest way to assure that your goal is attainable is to create one that you can break into smaller pieces, or objectives, and accomplish each and every part one by one if given the necessary time to do so. Additionally, since your goal should be broken into certain milestones, every time you complete one of the milestones, you will feel as though your effort counted for something, and you will feel motivated to continue working toward your goals. For example, if you are working toward stopping shutting down so often, you may tell yourself that you will have one less instance of anxious freezing than the day prior as your goal to strive for. This helps break down your goal into smaller, easier to handle portions that you can work toward without overwhelming yourself.

Realistic

Your goal absolutely must be realistic, or you will do nothing more than set yourself up to fail. It would be unrealistic and unacceptable to tell a native English speaker that he has one month to prepare for a court case that will be presented in Japanese, complete with writing out the documents in Japanese, without a translator. That is nearly impossible. Likewise, you should not assign impossible goals to yourself. Just because your friend, neighbor, sister, or spouse could achieve the goal you set does not mean that it is something you could realistically accomplish. People do not have the same inherent abilities or skills, and because of that, some people will never climb Mt. Everest, no matter how hard they try, and other people will never manage to write a bestselling novel. Your goal should be reasonable and realistic in comparison to your abilities while still giving you something to strive toward.

Timed

By setting a set amount of time to complete your goal, you provide yourself with yet another way to measure success. At the end of the time allotted, you will be able to analyze whether or not your goal has been achieved. This is better than leaving yourself with an indefinite end for your goal, as working with indefinite means you can consistently push off the goal further and further until you never actually complete it. When choosing a timeline for your goal, make sure that you set something that forces you to work toward the goal, but also that is attainable and realistic. You want to have a motivation to complete your goal, but you do not want that timeline to become another cause of stress for you.

Goal Exercise

Now that you understand what constitutes a SMART goal, it is time for you to put your knowledge to the test. Underline or highlight the goals that are SMART, and correct the ones that are not in order to make them SMART.

1. I will write a novel.
2. I will not be so angry when faced with challenges.
3. I will practice my affirmations every day in order to reduce how anxious I feel over the next month.
4. I will not have as many anxiety attacks next month.
5. I will meet new people
6. I will get on an airplane and travel to visit my family this October.

Goal Exercise Answer Key

1. I will write a novel in x amount of time, by writing y amount of words per day. (Any amount of time and any quantity of words is acceptable.)
2. When I face a challenge, I will try to remain calmer, eliminating my angry outbursts by x amount over y time. (Again, any amount and time is acceptable)
3. SMART goal. Example 3 should be underlined.
4. I will lessen my amount of anxiety attacks next month by x amount.

5. I will sign up for a new class to meet new people and attend weekly.

6. SMART goal. Example 6 should be underlined.

Step 1 Activity 1: Setting SMART Goals

Now that you understand what SMART goals are, it is time to form some of your own. Answer the following questions on a separate sheet of paper. Question 1 identifies what you want to see. Questions 2-6 help you make your desired results fit into SMART standards.

1. **The result I want:**

2. **Specific: Exactly what do I want to achieve to get the desired result?**

3. **Measurable: How do I know I have achieved it? What will I use to measure success?**

4. **Attainable: What steps do I need to complete to achieve my goal?**

5. **Realistic: Is the expected result realistic for me?**

6. **Timed: What is my deadline for achieving my desired result? How often will I work toward this goal?**

Using your answers to questions 2-6, reword your answer to question 1 to create a SMART goal.

My SMART goal is:

Step 1 Activity 2: Goal Planning

Your goal may feel difficult to achieve when you first create it, but remember, one of the components of SMART goals is making it attainable. For this activity, you will create a plan that will make your goal attainable. This involves breaking your goal into smaller objectives that are easier to attain and will help you take steps toward achieving your larger goal. Fill in the following categories to plan out how you will achieve your SMART goal, as well as identifying problems that may arise when trying to do so.

My SMART goal is:

What resources do I need to complete my goal?

What steps can I take to achieve my goal? What are my deadlines for each of these steps?
1.
2.
3.
4.
5.

What obstacles may arise?

How can I overcome these obstacles?

What will the results of achieving my goal look like?

Step 1 Activity 3: Tracking Progress

Tracking your progress through achieving your goals is one of the easiest ways to assure you are staying on track to completing your target goal on time. This form will use weeks as the measurement lengths, but you can alter this form to be daily or monthly, depending on the length of time you expect your objectives to take.

Date:
SMART Goal:

What are this week's objectives?

How successful were you in achieving this week's objectives? Why or why not?

If any, what obstacles did you face this week?

How can you overcome these obstacles?

Thoughts or reflections on this week's progress:

STEP 2: IDENTIFYING TRIGGERS

As previously discussed, emotional triggers are different stimuli that evoke powerful negative responses that are often disproportionate to the perceived slight. They often do not make sense to those observing the behaviors, and may not even make sense to you yourself. When you notice a pattern of being triggered on a regular basis, it is time to start identifying what those triggers are for you.

When triggered, the most common symptoms are:

- Feeling as though your heart is racing, with or without chest pain
- Feeling as though you are choking or cannot breathe
- Heat or cold flashes and sweating
- Nausea, dizziness, or faintness
- Shakiness or trembling
- Intense emotions
- Intense behavioral reactions intended to protect you from the intense emotions (yelling, running, crying, or other emotional reactions)

Why Emotional Triggers Occur

Oftentimes, triggers happen for one of three reasons, though others may crop up as well. The three most common reasons for emotional triggers are opposing beliefs or values, trauma, or to preserve the ego. Before continuing to learning to identify your triggers, you must first understand the three common reasons. When you understand these three common reasons, you will be able to sort each individual triggering event into a category that may help you make sense of it. For example, if your friend made a snide comment about a minority group when you promote equality, your strong reaction of being triggered likely falls into the first section of opposing viewpoints. That may bring you further understanding of why you would feel the need to react so strongly to such a small comment.

Opposing values and belief systems

We all hold a variety of beliefs that are integral to who we are as people. These could be religious beliefs or values related to who we are as people, such as a belief that all people deserve equal treatment, or that eating animals is wrong. You may hold those beliefs and accept them as true just the way they are, but inevitably, you will find someone else who disagrees with you.

When you feel like these beliefs you hold so deeply are being challenged by other people, you are likely to react viscerally in defense of them. After all, you accept them as true, so other people should, too. Your emotions run haywire as you defend them, feeling as though your own foundational beliefs and values are being challenged because it is easier to react defensively than it is to accept that those foundational beliefs, which you have used to build your entire life, are wrong.

Trauma

This is what most people typically think about when it comes to being "triggered." When people go through trauma, oftentimes, things reminiscent of the trauma can cause the same powerful emotions to come cascading down on the person who is triggered. Something as innocuous as a scent of food that happened to be baking during the traumatic event could cause the sufferer to feel as though he or she is stuck in the trauma all over again. These are also the most common triggers for people who suffer from PTSD. Anything that is reminiscent, no matter how coincidental, to the trauma trigger intense reactions.

Ego preservation

As discussed in the section about opposing beliefs, we do not like when foundational thoughts or beliefs are challenged. This is even more so when those thoughts and feelings challenge who we believe we are as people. The ego is the deepest sense of who you are that you hold. It is a sort of projection of who you are for other people; an idea of who you are supposed to be in society. This is built up with our thoughts, our culture, and cultural values, and other beliefs we hold in order to allow for us to fit in with our society. Ultimately, this ego serves as a way to protect ourselves from what we fear. In this instance, we fear the destruction of the ego that was created in order to protect us. Without that ego, we inherently feel vulnerable, and because of that, we will protect our egos viciously. When we feel as though our egos have been challenged or threatened, we respond strongly by becoming triggered. This triggered state allows for the threat to our egos to be fought off by any means necessary.

Identifying Emotional Triggers

Now that you understand the most frequent reasons for why you may feel emotionally triggered, you can begin to understand how to identify what specifically is triggering you.

This will require you to focus on introspection closely and to really consider what could possibly cause you to react so strongly. This process is not always easy, especially during periods during which you are triggered, as it is incredibly difficult to override the emotional part of your brain. However, once you do eventually learn to override the emotions wreaking havoc in your mind, you will be able to further understand why you sometimes behave the way you do.

The answers to what your triggers are may come as a surprise to you once they have been identified. When you are ready to start identifying your triggers, it is time to pull out your journal or prepare a quiet area and start reflecting.

Remember, this process should be done one trigger at a time so you can truly reflect on each one thoroughly and completely to identify as much information as you can about them on an individual level. After all, the only way you can hope to correct your triggers is if you understand them enough to desensitize yourself to them in the first place.

Identify your body's response

Think back to the last time you felt emotionally triggered: How did you feel? Maybe it started with tingling in your extremities, or your entire body running hot or cold before the heart palpitations started. Consider how you felt just as the triggered feelings began. This will help you identify what the triggers are in the future. If you are aware of the distinctive feelings in your body that precede the triggered emotions, you can use them as a cue to start calming yourself down or to remove yourself from the situation entirely in order to avoid the situation blowing up altogether. These physical responses are essentially your warning bells that things will get messy if you do not intervene somehow. Remember that even the most subtle reactions, even a slight change in your breathing pattern, could be a defining feature of when you are about to explode just as much as the more extreme reactions, such as raising a fist or taking an offensive posture to protect yourself. Any and all feelings and reactions you felt as you were triggered should be identified and recorded for future reference.

Identify your thoughts

After focusing on your body, it is time to turn your attention to your mind. Start to consider what thoughts went through your mind as you reacted so viscerally. Did you have thoughts about what the other person said or did? Did you think about a past trauma? Were you immediately subjected to a flashback? Did you think of how wrong that person was for saying that it is acceptable to eat animals when you are a vegan with strong feelings about animal rights? Or perhaps you found yourself wondering how someone could possibly be so dense as to not recognize that your religion is the right one no matter what and that some sort of evil has twisted the other person's mind. No matter what the thoughts that went through your mind were, make it a point to identify them. They can offer valuable insight into identifying what your triggers actually are. Oftentimes, these thoughts have to do with ego preservation or trying to preserve your beliefs or values from the other person's opposition.

Identifying the triggers

Now that you understand your physical and mental reactions to the trigger, you should be able to start to pinpoint exactly who or what was responsible for the trigger in the first place. Consider the three major causes for triggers: Opposing viewpoints, trauma, and ego protection. Most likely, the cause will fall into one of these three categories. It may have been a person who spoke specific words that reminded you of past trauma. Perhaps it was hearing that the other person disagreed with you and one of your deepest beliefs. Maybe you felt as though your own sense of self was being challenged or disregarded by another person, and that set you off. You may discover that something unexpected, such as the way someone words how he or she disagrees, may trigger a response you did not even know was possible, such as words reminding you of a third-grade teacher that you forgot, who used to punish you if you worded things a certain way. Think and reflect as long as necessary until you reach the heart of your feelings, and record any of the triggers that you discover during this period of reflection. You will likely be surprised to discover that you have many more triggers than you would initially guess and that those triggers are much more nuanced than you may have expected.

Identifying the circumstances behind the trigger

Some triggers require certain events or things to happen prior to them. You may have to be in a very specific mood for a trigger to bother you, or you may find that you are only triggered when you are hungry, sensitive, needing affection, or any other arbitrary reason. As irrational as these may sound, remember that feelings themselves are not rational, and that is okay. If there are prerequisites to your triggers, you need to understand them. By learning what these are, you will be able to be better prepared to handle a trigger that occurs.

In order to do this, you need to think about what occurred during the day prior to your trigger. Did you have a fight with your spouse? Were you already feeling anxious due to having an important meeting for work? Were your children particularly difficult that day? Once you understand what typically precedes you feeling triggered, you will be more mindful of your mental state and can remind yourself to calm down as necessary to prevent an explosion from happening before it is too late. This step may identify patterns for you that you never expected, such as realizing that your husband being away on a business trip, or your children needing more help to complete their schoolwork.

Identify unmet needs

Along with the three previously discussed causes of emotional triggers, oftentimes, there are some unmet needs underlying the reaction as well. These can each be assigned to the three categories, and when you can identify what needs you are missing when you become emotionally volatile, you can take the steps necessary to ensure that you are meeting all of your needs. These needs can be harder to identify than most of the other categories when trying to identify your triggers, but they can provide you with valuable insight. After all, if you know that underlying your triggers is a need to feel accepted, you will be able to remind yourself that you are accepted.

Here is a sample list of some of the common needs that are unmet when triggered. Think about which ones of these may be unmet when you feel triggered or emotionally volatile.

- Feeling accepted by those around you
- Having autonomy or the ability to make choices about your life
- Receiving positive attention from loved ones
- Feeling loved
- Feeling safe and secure in your environment and relationship
- Feeling as though you enjoy what you are doing and the people you are around
- Having a predictable routine that enables you to meet physical needs
- Feeling respected and valued

- Feeling relaxed or at ease
- Feeling desired or needed
- Feeling confident that you are making the right choices
- Feeling as though you are treated fairly
- Feeling that you have a sense of control over your environment and situation.

Step 2 Activity 1: Journaling Prompt

During your time completing this workbook, you will encounter multiple journaling prompts. These should be considered thoughtfully and completed as honestly as you can. Take a few moments to find a comfortable place to relax and free yourself from distractions. Get everything you will need and ensure you will not be interrupted. Your phone should be silenced, and you should shut your door and remind everyone in your home to leave you alone during this period.

Spend a minute breathing deeply and relaxing, trying to alleviate any tension you may feel and clear your mind, so your feelings prior to the journaling exercise do not cloud your mind or color your reflections. Consider the time you felt the most triggered. Take a minute to relive the event in your mind, going over the details. Answer the following questions:

What happened when you were triggered? Write a brief description of the circumstances.

How did you feel physically? Write down exactly how you remember your body reacted

What did you think about the situation at the moment?

What triggered this reaction?

What had happened the day you were triggered?

Did you have any unmet needs at that time?

How do you feel about the event now?

Step 2 Activity 2: Thought-Feeling-Action Charts

As you have learned through reading this far in the book, CBT focuses on the cycle in which thoughts, feelings, and actions influence each other in an endless loop. This activity has you identifying the thoughts, feelings, and actions behind your emotional triggers to further your understanding of what has caused them. You will complete three iterations of this cycle: The pre-triggered, triggered, and post-triggered iterations. After identifying these thoughts, feelings, and behaviors, you are tasked with reflecting on what the consequences to you being triggered were. Did you ruin a relationship? Lose a job? Upset someone? Whatever the result, write it down for future reference. Just as you did with the journal entry, make sure that you have no distractions present as you complete this activity.

Thoughts just before being triggered

Feelings just before being triggered

The behavior just before being triggered

Thoughts while triggered

Feelings while triggered

Behaviors while triggered

Thoughts after being triggered

Feelings after being triggered

Behaviors after being triggered

Were there any consequences to your behaviors?
How did you feel about these consequences?

Step 2 Activity 3: Identifying Common Anxiety Triggers

Triggers can be tricky to pin down if you are unsure where to start. Go over this list of common triggers and answer the following questions. When you are able to identify some of your triggers, you will be in a better position to work toward challenging them and restructuring your thinking to manage your anxiety. This activity has you looking at some of your common anxiety triggers and then analyzing your reaction to them, as well as why they trigger anxiety for you. Oftentimes, we simply accept our triggers without working to understand why they trigger anxiety, and it is important to understand why as well if we want to ever challenge and correct these triggers.

List of Common Anxiety Triggers

Crowds, Conflict or Confrontation, Embarrassment, Finances, Trauma, Violence, Familial Conflict, Social Interactions, Phones, Lack of Acceptance, Past Mistakes, Heights, Fear of Failing, Making Mistakes in the Future, Death, Trying New Activities, Change, Work, Accidents, Driving, Other People, Animals, Insects, Darkness, Illnesses, Being Trapped, Being Rejected, Feeling Useless or Stupid, Losing Loved Ones

List your three biggest anxiety triggers in the above list:

Why do these different scenarios or things cause you anxiety?

When was the last time you felt triggered by each of these?

How do you currently cope with your anxiety over these three triggers? How effective are your current coping mechanisms?

STEP 3: DESENSITIZING YOURSELF TO YOUR TRIGGERS

Ultimately, you react so volatilely to our emotional triggers because they hit a sensitive nerve somewhere. The trigger was something that bothered you so much that you could not help it: You lost control. Losing control is something that many people fear, and has been established repeatedly, is something that is associated with a lack of power. Feeling out of control is one of the most common triggers for feelings of anxiety, which means that the more you are triggered, the more likely you are to be triggered in the future as well as your anxiety continues to worsen over time. Luckily, there are ways to desensitize yourself from your trigger in order to regain control. These methods will focus on returning the power to yourself, shutting down the emotional part of your mind that demands control and returning that authority to the rational part of your brain instead. As you get more and more control over your triggers and your reactions to your triggers, you will likely find that you are triggered less often in general. This will result in a general improvement of your anxiety symptoms as a whole.

Now, you may be thinking, "Wow, that sounds perfect! How do I do that?" Unfortunately, the process will not be as easy as it sounds. You will be required to expose yourself to your trigger, likely repeatedly, in order to desensitize yourself. This is most frequently done through techniques such as exposure therapy, which seeks to introduce you to your anxiety triggers in a controlled environment in hopes of improving your reaction to said trigger when you realize it is not as bad as you initially assumed it would be. Keep in mind that exposure therapy is not always realistic alone, depending on your triggers. Some triggers, such as those involving two people, or that involve driving or other dangerous activities, may not be the smartest to attempt on your own as you may risk hurting yourself or others. If you do have a trigger that will require extra intervention, do not hesitate to ask a supportive friend, family member, or to find a therapist to help you through this process.

Remember that this process involves strong, difficult emotions, and being armed with methods to calm or soothe yourself, or people that you can trust to keep you calm and grounded will be particularly beneficial during your attempts to desensitize yourself. This step's activities will also aim to provide you with methods to help keep yourself calm and in control while you attempt this process. Remember to take your time and not to push yourself so far that you feel as though you would rather give up than work toward freeing yourself from your triggers' control. Do not forget to breathe as you go through the steps. Deep breaths will help you remain calm in the process, and if you can remain calm, you will be able to remain more in control of your feelings.

Exposure Therapy

Exposure therapy is exactly what it sounds like: You will repeatedly expose yourself to your trigger in a wide range of situations and circumstances in hopes of desensitizing yourself. This is especially helpful for phobias such as spiders or certain noises, and it can be tweaked to alleviate triggers to certain stimuli that were caused by trauma if done correctly. This process can be particularly emotional, as it involves you repeatedly willingly confronting some of your biggest fears or causes of anxiety, but it should help over time.

The first step to exposure therapy is to think of the idea of your trigger. For simplicity of explanations, consider a phobia of spiders. The trigger here is obviously spiders. In this step, you will be tasked with thinking about the idea of spiders. You do not have to visualize one, but just think about it. You likely already feel a mild triggered response: Your anxiety symptoms may start to manifest, and you feel your heart quickening at just the thought of a spider. This is normal. Throughout the next few days, randomly think about spiders every now and then. The goal is to do this so much that just thinking about them does not bring on an anxiety attack.

The next step is to visualize your trigger in your mind. For the arachnophobia person, visualize a spider in your mind. The idea of spiders is no longer triggering to you, but thinking about the spider's head, its jaws, and the way its legs move may cause a triggering response. Again, you feel the familiar symptoms of anxiety as you visualize the spider, building a web or skittering across a wall. Remind yourself that the spider cannot hurt you, as it is not even real, and that you are only thinking about how they look. Do this until it no longer triggers an immediate bout of anxiety. This may take a few days longer, but there will come a time where the image of a spider in your mind is no longer triggering.

Step three involves looking at actual photographs of your trigger. If spiders are your trigger, you need to pull up images either online or in books of different spiders. Let them be a variety of up close and from a distance, and pay attention to your body's response. If you still feel panic, you need to continue the exposure therapy. Continue to look at the spider, or whatever your trigger is, over a period of a few days until photographs no longer trigger your reaction.

Step four requires you to look at actual videos of your trigger. If spiders trigger intense anxiety, even a video may be distressing for you, even at this stage in the process. Set some time aside to watch videos of spiders doing spider things for a few minutes at a time throughout the day until you no longer feel triggered. As difficult as this process may feel in the moment, remind yourself that when you are no longer a slave to whatever your trigger is, you will agree it is worth the effort and stress.

Step five encourages you to encounter your trigger in real life. This can mean going up to look at a spider sitting on a web in a bush, or, if you are brave, going to a local pet store and gazing into the tarantula's tank. Do this until you no longer feel panic or triggered emotions when exposed to your trigger in real life.

Step six involves being actively involved with your trigger. If your trigger is driving, this would be the day you finally drive on your own. If it is confrontation or conflict, you make it a point to stand up for yourself. If your trigger is spiders, you may allow for one to climb on you in a controlled environment, such as at a pet store or a zoo in which interaction with the animals is encouraged. When you engage your trigger in real life, you should find that by this point, your reaction to it is much more muted than it had been when you first began this process to overcome and desensitize yourself. Congratulations! Once you complete this stage, you have more-or-less completed do-it-yourself exposure therapy.

When your trigger is something a little more complicated, such as men after a sexual assault, or a certain sound that you relate to a traumatic event, exposure therapy can seem impossible, as you may initially think that you would have to repeatedly expose yourself to sexual assault or the trauma all over again. However, that is not necessarily the case. Let us first look at what exposure therapy for a person afraid of men might look like.

First, the victim would be encouraged to think about the idea of men, or even the particular feature, quirk, saying, or behavior that the victim associates with the trauma. Perhaps the attacker had a beard, and now the victim is triggered every time a man with a beard goes by. The first step would be to consider the idea of a beard. From there, it would be to visualize a beard. The victim would then move toward looking at pictures of beards, then men with beards, followed by videos of men with beards, and ultimately, encouraged to engage with men with beards to desensitize him or herself to that particular trigger.

Likewise, the person who feels triggered at a specific sound would be encouraged to think about the concept of the sound and what causes it. Once that has been completed, the person would hear the sound with his or her mind, before then seeking to listen to a recording of the sound, followed by a video of the sound being caused. Eventually, he or she would work up to being present while the sound happens nearby, and maybe even to cause the sound him or herself if it is something that is possible.

Nearly any kind of trigger can be identified and eventually desensitized with a little bit of creativity and effort. However, if you ever feel like your trigger is insurmountable, or that you are unequipped to handle it yourself, please seek aid from a medical professional. Someone licensed to help you will be far more able to handle your emotions than a book that cannot provide you active feedback or customized support.

If you are struggling but still feel able to work through exposing and desensitizing yourself, remember that it is difficult. The process is by no means easy, and you will likely have moments of wanting to quit or try another method to control your anxiety. Rest assured that it will get easier with time and that with perseverance, you will overcome these anxiety triggers. If it were easy, you would not be sitting in front of this book, seeking help in the first place. Do not give up, no matter how tempting it may seem, and do not forget that you are strong enough to get through this, regardless of whether it is by yourself or with a professional. What is important is the end result of you feeling more able to handle your emotional triggers. How you get there is less important than the results, and you are no less successful if you do require extra support.

Remember, as you go about this process, you should be reminding yourself what your end goal is. You are setting these goals for yourself in an effort to better yourself. When you are no longer being triggered, you will feel less anxious in general, even when exposed to those things that typically would trigger you.

Step 3 Activity 1: Exposure Therapy Activity Plan

As discussed, exposure therapy is one of the most efficient ways to desensitize yourself to your emotional triggers. This activity will encourage you to create an action plan to begin desensitizing yourself. You will outline your plan step by step, so you have an idea of what to expect during the next several days or weeks as you attempt to desensitize yourself. You should first answer the questions at the beginning, followed by writing out what each step will look like. After you have eventually managed to work through all of the steps, reflect on the results.

What is your trigger?

Why does it trigger you?

Step 1: Thinking about the concept

Step 2: Visualizing the trigger

Step 3: Looking at still shots of the trigger

Step 4: Watching videos of the trigger

Step 5: Observing the trigger in real time

Step 6: Engaging with your trigger

After completing Steps 1-6, do you feel more capable of addressing your trigger? How do you feel now?

Step 3 Activity 2: Worst Case Scenario Roleplay

When you are trying to get through the steps of desensitizing yourself, it can be helpful to engage in what is called a worst-case scenario roleplay. In this, you will consider what the worst that could happen is when you face your trigger or fear. This can help you recognize that your fear or expectation that is the root behind your trigger is not true, which can help you assuage some of those feelings of anxiety.

For example, assume you are triggered by dogs. Perhaps you were bitten by a dog once as a child and have been terrified of them ever since. You may be working your way through exposure therapy, but finding yourself frightened too much to continue. You have found yourself stuck at step 5, seeing a dog in person. Ask yourself, "What is the worst thing that could happen if I engage with this dog?" In this case, the worst-case scenario is that the dog will bite or be aggressive in some way. Then, ask yourself, how likely is that to happen again? The answer is not likely at all. With that reminder that the worst-case scenario is not likely to occur, you should then feel a little bit better and move forward. When you see that the worst-case scenario did not happen, you remind yourself to not think the worst of every situation.

In a journal or with some friends, fill in the following about one of your emotional triggers. After engaging with your trigger, return to this assignment and record the results of facing it.

What is the worst thing that could happen if you face your trigger?

How likely is that?

Results:

Step 3 Activity 3: Mindfulness Grounding Activity

Mindfulness is focusing on the present moment in a detached, emotionless manner. When engaging in mindfulness, you should seek to look at things rationally, which oftentimes does require you to step away from your emotions. In order to do this, you must focus on your feelings and acknowledge them. Recognize that they are there, but do not act upon them. The point of this is to enable you to recognize when you are being triggered so you can stop it. When you are feeling overwhelmed or triggered, try this activity to help you regain control of your emotions. Achieving this step is easiest with the following grounding activity:

First, identify five things you can see around you. Take a deep breath between each thing you identify.

Second, touch four things around you. Focus on their textures as you again take a deep breath between each item.

Third, listen to three different sounds you can identify around you. Focus on each different sound and describe them to yourself between deep breaths.

Fourth, identify two scents in the air. Take in deep breaths and hold them as you identify the scents.

Lastly, identify one taste in your mouth or in the air.

STEP 4: IDENTIFYING CORE BELIEFS

Core beliefs were defined earlier in the book, but as a quick refresher, these are the innermost beliefs you hold about yourself. They involve how you see yourself and influence how you behave, as you ultimately feel locked into these core beliefs. Behaving in a way that you do not associate with your core beliefs can lead to episodes of feeling emotionally triggered, as to deny a core belief would be to challenge your ego. Remember, you desperately try to protect your ego at all costs, and that ego is built upon your own core beliefs.

These core beliefs are largely unconscious unless you go through the effort of identifying them, so recognizing them on their own can be particularly tricky. However, they are important to know for future steps in the CBT process. You need to be able to analyze whether or not your core beliefs are negative or are distorted later on in order to complete the cognitive restructuring process. These thoughts about yourself influence everything: If you feel as though you are not worthy of compassion, you will never go easy on yourself when you make a mistake. Every mistake will be grievous and horrendous, and no one will be able to convince you otherwise, even if you would never judge someone so harshly for the same mistake. You would absolutely, wholeheartedly agree that the other person deserves to be treated with grace and that the mistake is no big deal. However, you would never show yourself that compassion, and you would expect those around you to treat you as harshly as you treat yourself due to your own current core beliefs. That core belief, the belief that you are unworthy of compassion, will permeate everywhere in your life if you do not identify and correct it. Left unchallenged, that core belief will be left to fester and spread to more and more aspects of your life, ruining whatever it can touch and infecting more of your life with that toxic negativity.

Introspection

In order to identify your core beliefs, you must be able to identify your feelings and thoughts and then identify why those thoughts are so important to you. Pretend for a moment that you felt really disappointed today that you were late to work, breaking your previously perfect attendance record. You felt really upset and beat yourself up over being three minutes late one time during the last several years you have worked there. Pay attention to this feeling of disappointment, as it is an important key to one of your core beliefs.

Perhaps, in your disappointment, you told yourself, "See? Look how useless I am. I can't even make it work on time. I should have left a few minutes earlier to accommodate for bad traffic. Instead, I didn't. I'm such a lame, invaluable employee, and I don't deserve this job. In fact, I'll probably be let go at my next review." Anyone around you may see this as a particularly unwarranted response toward yourself, especially with a perfect attendance record.

Things happen, and you know you would not judge any of your coworkers harshly over being late for something out of their control. Rationally, somewhere deep down, you may know that your coworkers also would not treat you poorly for being understandably late, but that realization is buried deep underneath a core belief of yours. In order to uncover that core belief, you need to break down your mental diatribe toward yourself. Each time you uncover another reason that you use to justify it, you must continue to ask yourself why that matters. The idea is to understand the underlying beliefs that are coloring the way you treat yourself.

Ask yourself why you would say all of that to yourself. Your answer may look like, "Because I'm so useless, and I'll get fired for being late. Only useless or deadbeat employees are late to work."

With that answer in mind, ask yourself why that matters. Why do you feel like a useless employee? Perhaps your answer looks like, "Because I can't even make it work on time and that's a basic part of the job description."

Probe yourself further. Ask why you feel like you cannot make it work on time. "Because I'm incapable of planning ahead or for emergencies or unforeseen circumstances."

Finally, you have arrived at an answer relevant to you: You feel as though you are incapable. Thinking you are incapable of is your core belief in this situation. That one tiny belief that you may have been unaware of prior to this moment colored the entire situation and sent your anxiety on overdrive. Someone without feeling as though he or she was incapable would likely not have thought twice of being late to work once over the course of several years. Your supervisors are human too and would likely have the compassion to excuse unforeseen circumstances such as an accident or a car malfunctioning as valid reasons to be late to work. After all, you cannot control whether there was an accident on the route to the office.

This process can be completed for any thoughts. Some core beliefs will be easier than others to uncover, but do not feel discouraged if you feel like you are not making progress. This can be a long process, but when you understand how your thoughts are working against you, making your life more difficult and causing you to treat yourself with little compassion, you will be better prepared to begin changing those negative beliefs. Have faith that understanding the innermost parts of your mind and thoughts will enable you to understand your behaviors better than ever before.

You should also be prepared to reveal some of your most intimate vulnerabilities during this process. You will reveal parts of you that you never knew were there, and that can be scary and difficult to process. Remember that seeing those vulnerabilities is the only way you can ever hope to truly remedy them, no matter how difficult it may be. You may realize that parts of your life that you never expected to have left a lasting impact actually defined you more than parts of your life you considered integral.

Keep in mind that this process should be completed one at a time, with you seeking to understand one core belief at a time before moving on to the next one. When you are able to focus on one at a time, you can give yourself the time that you need to truly identify each core belief without feeling rushed or pressured.

Over time, maybe over a period of weeks or even months, you will manage to identify some of your most deeply buried core beliefs, and with that knowledge comes the control over your mind.

Step 4 Activity 1: Journaling Prompt to Identify Core Beliefs

For this activity, you are tasked with journaling with the goal of identifying a core belief. This activity can be completed as many times as you desire to identify all sorts of core beliefs you may be unaware of, but at the bare minimum, it is recommended that you complete this for each of the major conflicts or negative feelings you have had in life recently to identify the core beliefs hiding within them. Again, remember to keep your journaling environment free from distractions and comfortable as you complete this activity.

Identify your most recent negative thought toward yourself. Describe the circumstances around it in detail.

Think about your negative thought and write down why you think you have it. Be as thorough as you can to discuss how it is relevant to your life and the impact you feel like it has had on your life.

Did you learn anything about yourself during this journal prompt? Did you uncover a core belief? If so, what was it?

Step 4 Activity 2: "Why?" Challenge

This step will mimic the structure used to identify core beliefs in this chapter. You will identify a negative feeling and identify the circumstances around it repeatedly until you reach the core belief underlying it. Every action and behavior have a core belief rooted somewhere deep down within it if you engage in enough introspection. For this activity, it will be easiest to track if you write it down in your journal or on a piece of scratch paper so you can watch your thought train grow and follow it to the end result.

Identify a recent time you felt a negative emotion.

What happened to make you feel that way?

Why is that relevant? Why does it matter? Ask yourself this question until you arrive at a statement about yourself that identifies how you see yourself.

What is the core belief you identified?

Was this core belief a surprise to you? Why or why not?

Step 4 Activity 3: Core Belief Reflection Activity

Now that you have identified some of your core beliefs, it is time to reflect on them so you can see how they impact your feelings and behaviors. This activity will require you to analyze how one of your core beliefs impacts a significant amount of your life, even in areas where you and your beliefs are irrelevant. One little core belief about yourself impacts how you see the world around you, as well as your view of the future. Once you have filled out your views of yourself, the world, and the future, it is time for you to analyze the results. Are you happy with what you wrote down? Why or why not? Then consider what answers you would prefer to see instead. Remember to be as honest as you can during this activity.

Identify one of your core beliefs

Describe yourself through the view of your core belief.

Describe the world through the view of your core belief.

Describe how you see the future going through the view of your core belief.

Do you like what you wrote down? Why or why not?

What results do you want to see in the above categories?

STEP 5: IDENTIFYING NEGATIVE THINKING AND COGNITIVE DISTORTIONS

Once you have identified your underlying core beliefs, you are ready to start identifying whether they are negative automatic thoughts or cognitive distortions. While these two concepts are similar, there are small nuances that differ the two that you should be sure to brush up on prior to completing this step.

This step will have you analyze your core beliefs, one by one, checking them past the provided lists and criteria to decide if they fall into negative automatic thoughts or cognitive distortions. If they fall into either, you know they are thoughts that are not beneficial to you or productive in any way, shape, or form. This is critical, as it will provide you with concrete reasons to define your thoughts and provide you a reason to change them. If you can actively identify which of your thoughts are unhealthy or unproductive, you will better be able to identify which ones require you to change them in order to fix your mindset. Remember, these negative and distorted thoughts influence your feelings and behaviors, and cause your feelings and behaviors to become just as negative and hurtful as these thoughts, so changing them will always be in your best interest. The first step to changing them is by identifying them.

Common Negative Automatic Thoughts

Negative automatic thoughts, as defined earlier, are automatic thoughts that occur unconsciously and are oftentimes ignored, but accepted as fact. They color your perceptions of yourself and the way you interact with the world. When trying to identify whether thoughts are negative, you may struggle with thoughts that do not outwardly appear negative. Or, you may think that some of your negative thoughts are not necessarily harmful. After all, negativity is a natural part of being human. We all have negative thoughts from time to time. When trying to identify whether your thoughts are negative, you should consider whether or not that thought is beneficial to you in any way.

For example, imagine that you have a core belief that any effort you put forth in order to control your anxiety is useless. Stop and consider whether that thought is beneficial in any way. Does it help you to hold that thought? Does that thought make you feel better or worse about your situation? If you do not think it is beneficial to you, regardless of whether it is true or not, or whether you believe it or not, it may be a negative thought that requires restructuring for you to get out of the rut of negativity. Remember, those negative thoughts will sour your mood and make you behave in more negative ways.

Common Cognitive Distortions

Cognitive distortions are more than just negative thoughts, though they are most often negative. They are usually false. Something about them just does not make sense. Much like how you can have fallacies in logic that automatically disqualify the argument, you have cognitive distortions that will invalidate your core beliefs and thoughts. Take your time to analyze and really absorb the most common kinds of cognitive distortions. When you have an idea of what to expect, you can more accurately identify when they are occurring, which will help you to recognize that the thoughts you are having are distorted, and therefore, should not be trusted.

Blame

Oftentimes, we find ways to use blame to either cause or avoid guilt. When you are using blame, you often think in terms of should or should not, or must or must not. The problem with these conditional words; however, is that when they fail, they result in feeling guilt or a sense of not being good enough. This can quickly become catastrophic as you blame yourself for failing, and that guilt you feel only further solidifies your blame, while negatively influencing your feelings and behaviors, which will likely result in more of the same failures, over and over again. For example, say that you suffer from social anxiety. You promise your friend that you absolutely will go with her to the party this weekend. When the weekend comes, your anxiety starts building up because you know you should go to the party because you promised. However, as this anxiety builds up, you eventually cave and decide not to go, leaving you with all of the guilt associated with letting your friend down. That guilt may make you feel as though you are a bad friend, which only further exacerbates your social anxiety. Instead of motivating yourself with your conditional expectation and obligation, you have demotivated yourself and made the problem worse.

Catastrophizing

This distortion always involves immediately jumping to the worst-case scenario and assuming that it will occur. No matter how unrealistic that worst case scenario is, you automatically assume that will happen. For example, if your friend went on a trip, but never texted you upon landing safely at the airport at the scheduled time, you immediately assume something bad happened on the plane, imagining it crashing on the runway or disappearing over the ocean as opposed to the more logical assumption of her phone dying during the trip. You spend the next several hours scouring the internet for any sources that mention your friend's plane crash, and when that turns up nothing, you assume that your friend got kidnapped, held up by immigration, or even hit by a car in the airport parking lot. All of those scenarios seem more realistic to you than the simple assumption that your friend's phone died. To an outsider, this is clearly illogical, but to you at the moment, you cannot help but assume the worst.

Emotional reasoning

In contrast to rational thinking is emotional thinking. This form of thinking appeals to your emotions, allowing them to rule over your judgment. There is a reason that emotional reasoning is a sort of oxymoron: The two are incompatible. When you allow your emotions to rule over your rational part of your brain, you will not be able to make truly rational decisions. Instead, you will rely on our emotions as justification for whatever distortion you hold. Remember that emotions are fickle and constantly changing: This means that your emotional reasoning will be changing every time your mood changes.

For example, consider the idea that you feel anxious about going up in front of your coworkers to lead an important meeting about a project that your department completed. You know that you feel anxious, and that anxiety precedes bad things happening. With that emotional feeling, you decide that you will fail your presentation because you feel anxious. There is nothing indicating that you will fail aside from that anxiety you feel, and unfortunately, that anxiety makes you more likely to fail. This creates a sort of self-defeating prophecy in which you let your negative emotions guide you, only to confirm their validity because of those negative emotions. Remind yourself that just because you may feel anxious today does not mean that something back will happen. You may feel differently tomorrow, so do not allow your feelings today to dissuade you from trying your best. Do not dwell on those negative feelings as they will most likely pass.

Focusing on the negative

This is exactly what it sounds like: When your thought is taking the distortion of focusing on the negative, you ignore all of the positive in favor of letting the negative define your experience or perception. No matter how little the negative might happen compared to the positive, you will look to the negative to pass judgment. For example, if you occasionally argue with your spouse, as spouses do, you may get so caught up in the occasional arguments that you allow them to color your perception of the entire relationship. While you may have had an argument that made you feel as though you and your spouse are incompatible because you fight, you do not recognize that after the argument, your spouse asked to play your favorite game with you, or got your favorite take out for dinner in a sort of peace offering. All of the ways you and your spouse are compatible seem irrelevant in comparison to your occasional arguments, and you let that negativity overshadow the vast amount of positive interactions and feelings in the relationship. Because you dwell on the negativity, you see every individual argument as more and more evidence that your relationship will fail. When you think it will fail, you obviously would not be putting in the effort your relationship needs, and if your spouse ever decides that your negativity has gone on too far and does leave you, you will point to every trivial argument as justification that you were never compatible, to begin with instead of recognizing that your own negativity drove your spouse to end the marriage.

Focusing on regret

When you focus on the past and all the things you could have done differently, you keep yourself in a mindset of regret. Instead of seeing things in the past that did not go according to plan as learning experiences that can teach you what not to do next time, you dwell on what you did wrong. You constantly think of ways you could have fixed the problem at that moment instead of ways that you could learn from your mistake and do better in the future. This does two things: It leaves you feeling intense guilt and regret, and also keeps your mindset in the past, which is not productive in fixing your thoughts or behaviors.

To further illustrate this concept, consider a situation in which you got into a car accident. The other driver was drunk and crashed into the passenger side of your car. No one was seriously injured, but you were out of work for a week for car repairs and to allow your minor injuries and aches and pains to heal. You need your car for daily tasks at work, but it was so damaged that it was totaled, and even with insurance, you did not receive enough money to cover the costs of getting a new car that you could use for your job. Because you had no car for an extended period of time, you missed more work, and ultimately, you had to use the insurance payout just to cover your bills, and you lost your job.

Now, this is an extremely unlucky occurrence, but it was not your fault. You were following all of the rules of the road, but the other person was drunk and hit you. Rather than recognizing that you had no fault, you instead focused on all the ways things could have been different. You wonder if you should have left work on time instead of ten minutes late to avoid the encounter, or that you should have seen the car veering into your lane when you were driving and reacted quicker. You should have had better savings stash so being out of work temporarily would not have cost you your job due to finances. Rather than looking at how you could learn, or in this case, recognizing that this was not your fault in any way, shape, or form, you focus on regret and continue to demean and belittle yourself over something that you cannot change. It is a waste of your energy to focus on the past when it will not fit your current situation.

Labeling

This simple distortion focuses on name-calling. However, just because it is simple does not mean it is harmless. Name-calling will not fix your problems, nor is it a healthy way to cope with stress or unforeseen circumstances. Oftentimes, core beliefs rooted in labeling are calling yourself things, such as saying, "I am unlovable," or "I am stupid and worthless." These labels do nothing more than label you and do not help you in any way. You get so caught up in your own beliefs and negative labels that you find yourself unable to prove them wrong. For example, if you believe that you are unlovable, you will likely act with low self-esteem, which may push away anyone who does love you or wants to be with you. The fact that you pushed them away with your lack of self-confidence only further iterates to yourself that you are unlovable when in reality, the problem was that you were so demanding and needy that the other person felt overwhelmed and unable to keep up. In this case, your label of being unlovable crippled you, ruining potential relationships that would have proven that label wrong.

Mind reading

Oftentimes, we assume we know exactly what someone else is thinking. You may feel like you know just by looking at the other person. Usually, whatever thought you are assuming is true is negative in some way, shape, or form, and is most frequently related to you somehow. For example, you may assume that your best friend really only pities you and hangs out with you as a sort of good gesture and out of the kindness of his heart, rather than recognizing that your friend likely sees the best in you and therefore wants to be around you to enjoy your personality. You assume this is true just because you think it is, and act in that fashion. So, if you feel like your friend does not truly see you as a best friend the way he says he does, you will constantly be leery when he offers you something or asks to hang out, thinking there has to be an ulterior motive in there somewhere because no one would ever want to willingly hang out with someone like you. Remember, you are not a mind reader, so you have no way of identifying these thoughts as true, so you should not dwell on them. Take people's word at face value because they are the only ones privy to their thoughts, no matter how sure you may be of them.

Predicting the future

With this cognitive distortion, you predict that bad things will happen. Similar to catastrophizing and focusing on the negative, you assume that the bad thing will happen, and because of that, you may find yourself avoiding attempting things you should out of fear of failing. You do not want to fail, so you instead opt not to attempt it at all, feeling like the only way to win is to not engage.

For example, if you feel as though you will fail at a job interview, you may decide not to go at all to save yourself the embarrassment. This is somewhat ironic, however, as by refusing to at least try to complete whatever you fear you will fail at, you have failed by omission. Because you did not try at all, you upped your chances of failing to achieve your goal to 100%.

Taking it personally

When you make things personal, you assume that everything negative around you has to do with you somehow. If your spouse is stressed out or quieter than usual, you assume he or she is upset with you. If your boss was short with you at the coffee stand, it is because you are failing at your job and will be fired soon.

If your friend does not message you back immediately, you wonder if you upset them. Instead of recognizing that you likely had nothing to do with any of their negative moods, you have inserted yourself as the cause.

This can happen with total strangers as well: If the cashier is short with you, you may assume that you said something offensive as opposed to considering that he might have some familial problems at home, or be worrying about finals next week.

Remind yourself that you are not responsible for everyone else's feelings, and no matter how sure you are that you are the root of everyone else's problems, remind yourself that the world does not revolve around you and you should not put such a heavy burden on your shoulders.

Your spouse may have had an argument with a coworker. Your boss could have received bad news about a family member's health. Your friend's phone's battery could be dead. None of those is your fault.

Thinking in black and white

When you think of black and white, you refuse to acknowledge that there is a grey area in all things. You see things as exactly right or exactly wrong with no middle ground. This is a problem, however, as everything in the world has nuances and shades of grey, and forcing yourself to think in extremes only serves to set yourself up for failure. When you think in extremes, you may feel as though you are a failure if you fail even once with a wide range of successes. After all, one failure means you are not perfect 100% of the time, and that lack of perfection is enough to deem you as a failure if you define things as true or false or black and white. Oftentimes, these distortions will involve using words such as always, never, all, none, or other absolutes. To illustrate this example, imagine that you have a core belief of, "I always fail when I attempt to alleviate my anxiety." Every time you have an anxiety attack, you use it as proof that you are a failure, no matter how much you may have reduced the frequency of your anxiety attacks.

Unable or unwilling to disconfirm

When you are unwilling or unable to disconfirm something, you are unable to accept that one of your beliefs may be wrong. You instead live in a state of denial, in which you ignore and reject every single thing that could possibly contradict you, or you force them to somehow justify your distorted beliefs, even if the process of using a disproving piece of evidence would win you the gold medal in mental gymnastics. For example, you may feel as though you are a bad spouse. Every time your spouse compliments you or tells you that you are the perfect partner for him or her, you automatically disregard it. You may even tell yourself that the only reason your partner is complimenting you is to convince you to stick around and out of pity because you are such a poor partner. Rather than taking the compliment and accepting it graciously, you twist it into some sort of slight or insult, forcing even the kindest of words to fit into your distorted narrative. It is easier for you to use that distortion to prove yourself right than it is to accept that you may have been wrong.

Unfairly comparing

It is unfair to compare yourself to other people. They have completely different background stories and measures of success. Each person is different, and because of that, comparing yourself to others is a surefire way to cause yourself mental duress. Just as you would never compare apples to strawberries to decide which is best in your recipe for blueberry pie because they are all such drastically different fruits that will create different results, you should not seek to compare yourself to other people. Remember that you are not built the same. You did not have the same opportunities, challenges, and capabilities as the other person. It is unfair to judge your life, your success, and your value based upon the standards for another person. All you will do is set yourself up to feel bad about yourself, as you are most likely comparing yourself to someone who has everything you want instead of someone who has less than you. If you dwell on other people's experiences and particular situations, you only serve to waste your own mental energy that could be spent bettering your own situation.

How to Identify Negative Thoughts and Cognitive Distortions

Now that you have lists of what constitutes a negative thought or cognitive distortion, you can begin comparing your own list of thoughts and core beliefs to the above cheat sheets. Any time you think one may be a cognitive distortion or negative thought, you should closely analyze it to see if it fits any of the above criteria and mark it for further challenging, which will be completed in Step 6: Cognitive Restructuring. The activities for this step will help you further decide whether your thoughts and beliefs are in need of restructuring.

Step 5 Activity 1: Journaling Prompt

This section will have your journal to uncover some of your core beliefs and thoughts so you can use your journal as a sort of guide to begin labeling them as negative thoughts or cognitive distortions. Just as before, set yourself up in a quiet area, free from distractions, and free write. Today's topic is on negative thoughts and will involve two parts.

Part 1: Set a timer for 5 minutes, and write until it beeps.

How do you see your personality? Describe yourself as though you were a character in a book.

Part 2: Go over your description of yourself and identify any negative thoughts or cognitive distortions within it.

Did any of the negative thoughts or cognitive distortions surprise you? Why or why not? How do you feel about them?

Step 5 Activity 2: Identifying Distortion or Negativity Traps

This activity involves identifying which situations and thoughts lead you to think traps. These traps will be your cognitive distortions or negative thoughts. Answer the following questions for three different situations in order to identify your thinking traps.

Describe a difficult situation that happened this week:

Name a few automatic thoughts that came up during that situation:

Identify how those automatic thoughts made you feel:

What thinking traps or cognitive distortions did these thoughts fall into?

Step 5 Activity 3: Automatic Thoughts Log

Throughout the day, identify any automatic thoughts that come up. After feeling something negative, take a moment to log it down in a journal using the following format. When writing down what happened, be sure to include what happened to you, as well as your reactions. At the end of the day, look over your log and try to identify any patterns within it.

Date:
Time:
Location:
Feeling:
What happened:

What underlying automatic thoughts can you identify?

Are there any patterns to when you feel negative feelings or have negative or distorted thoughts?

STEP 6: COGNITIVE RESTRUCTURING

Now that you understand the various types of triggers, negative thoughts, and cognitive distortions that may be causing the bulk of your emotional distress, you are ready to begin the process of cognitive restructuring. Remember the cycle that was introduced earlier in the book between thoughts, feelings, and behaviors. Imagine that cycle is negative, and consider all the ways it may impact your life. Now, imagine what would happen if you reshape that cycle to be positive.

Cognitive restructuring is the foundation of CBT, and now that you are able to identify all of the types of thoughts that would require restructuring, you can begin the process. This is a multifaceted goal, and it does require significant effort on your part. Think of how difficult it is to break a bad habit: it takes plenty of time, but eventually, you see the results. When you begin restructuring your thinking, you need to get yourself in the habit of thinking in a positive manner instead of a negative one. This can be done through a variety of ways, challenging your thoughts, reminding yourself that your thoughts are false, or inserting affirmations. The more you get into the habit of challenging the negative thoughts and core beliefs, the easier it will be to deny them.

Creating Affirmations

One of the single most beneficial tools in the process of cognitive restructuring will be creating affirmations and using them on a regular basis, both to ground yourself at the moment when you are feeling your anxiety threatening to take over, and during the day as a habit. Affirmations are short phrases or sentences that you can use to keep yourself stable or remind yourself of something during moments of weakness. Creating affirmations is relatively simple, but it does require you to follow three key criteria to create an effective affirmation.

About yourself

The most important part of your affirmation is to ensure it is about yourself. You can only control yourself and your reactions, and you only know your own thoughts, so focusing your affirmation on being about yourself pushes it to be something that you can influence to make it true. By reminding yourself that you are strong, or patient, or in control, you put the veracity of the affirmation on yourself and make it something that you yourself can confirm. If you were to make your statement about other people, such as, "My family loves me," you could prove that wrong by reminding yourself that you are not a mind reader, and you should never presume to know what is going on inside someone else's mind. That makes an opening for you to deny the validity of your affirmation, which means that it would not be very effective.

Present-focused

The second key component of your affirmation is to assure that it is written in the present tense. By writing your affirmation in the past tense, you would say that your affirmation may have been true in the past, but that leaves room for you to deny the validity in the present or future. Likewise, saying you will do something leaves you with an opening to not do it at that moment. By focusing on the particular moment, you are in, you are asserting to yourself that it is true as you speak. This again returns control to yourself and enables you to use the affirmation to ground yourself.

Positive

The third key component of your affirmation is to assure it is positive. Just as CBT itself focuses on the positive, you should assure that your affirmations are worded in a positive form in order to keep your thinking in positives. Consider the difference between saying, "I do not yell when I am mad," and, "I remain calm in the face of anger." Between the two, the second one is more motivating and keeps your mind thinking positively while the other denies an action. Just as you should keep your goals positive, you want to keep your affirmations positive as well. This also reminds you of what you are or should be doing as opposed to what you should be avoiding, which can serve as a fantastic reminder of how to get yourself out of the anxious feelings.

Examples

With those three components in mind, you are ready to begin forming your own affirmations. Here are some examples relevant to handling anxiety.

- I am capable of achieving what I need to do to get through my day.
- I will breathe deeply to calm myself, even in the face of anxiety.
- I am worthy of the same compassion and consideration I give to other people.
- I am lovable and good enough. I love myself the way I am.
- I can get through these tough times, even though it is difficult.
- I am strong enough to manage my anxiety.
- I am in control of myself.
- I am physically safe, even when my anxiety tries to convince me otherwise.
- I have the mental clarity to see through the tricks my anxiety tries to pull, and the strength to continue through my day despite those tricks.

Using Affirmations

With your affirmations chosen, you are prepared to start using them on a regular basis. The idea that you should keep in mind is reciting affirmations to yourself on a specific schedule. Eventually, they will become automatic habits, and the more you say them to yourself, the more you will convince yourself that they are true. For example, if you drive to work every day, decide that you will recite one of your affirmations every day as you buckle yourself in and drive down your home road. You may decide to recite another every morning as you brush your teeth. Try to recite one or two of your affirmations at least ten times at a time a few times a day so they soon become habitual thoughts. You will know you have succeeded when you begin to recite them to yourself on a regular basis without prompting them. At that point, they are well on their way to becoming automatic thoughts of their own, and they will begin to influence your behaviors and feelings in ways you never thought were possible.

Mindfulness

Mindfulness is useful here yet again, and through your affirmations, you can achieve it. If you feel your anxiety growing, and realize you are teetering toward being emotionally triggered by your thoughts or feelings, you can begin to ground yourself in order to gain the clarity you need to challenge your anxious feelings. Along with the grounding technique introduced earlier in this book, you can use your affirmations to trigger that state. By creating an affirmation related to clarity and control, you can remind yourself to sort of dissociate yourself from your roiling emotions so you can begin to look at things logically. By looking at things logically and interrupting your anxiety before it can reach a full-fledged anxiety attack, you will be able to begin challenging whether or not it is actually worthy of the response you are giving it. Once you have achieved this mindfulness, you can analyze your response.

You will be able to ask yourself why you are responding the way you are, as well as if you are acting in a logical, positive manner. If not, you will have the mental clarity needed to interrupt yourself and behave positively. This is not an easy feat, but the more you are able to stop your emotions from ruling you, the more you will create better habits that will lead toward the process of cognitive restructuring.

Ultimately, combining these two ways to go about cognitive restructuring will be the most effective. By using techniques during your day-to-day life as well as when you are having anxiety attacks, you are attacking your symptoms two separate ways, doubling your effort and the results. Soon, you will find that your anxiety symptoms wane and you are better able to cope with the small things that used to scare you or trigger negative emotions. In time, you will feel as though your anxiety is in control, and that you are able to manage your symptoms on your own.

Step 6 Activity 1: Affirmation Plan

Remembering the rules for the structure of affirmations, create some affirmations for various situations that are positive, present-focused, and about yourself that will be useful to you and your anxiety. Commit to a time every day that you will recite your affirmation at least 10 times. After the first day, come back and reflect on how it affected your day. Revisit this assignment after one week and reflect on how it has affected your week.

Identify a situation that is triggering:
Create an affirmation for that situation:
When will you use this affirmation?

Identify a negative thought you hold:
Create an affirmation to negate that thought:
When will you use this affirmation?

Identify a cognitive distortion you hold:
Create an affirmation to challenge this distortion:
When will you use this affirmation?

Create an affirmation that you will use to ground yourself when your anxiety is high:

How will you use this affirmation to ground yourself when triggered?

After one day of using your affirmations, did you notice any changes? How do you feel about them?

After one week of using your affirmations, did you notice any changes? How do you feel about them? Did they help you?

Step 6 Activity 2: Challenging Negative and Distorted Thoughts

This activity will have you choose a negative thought or a cognitive distortion and answer a series of questions about it in order to invalidate it. As you go through these questions, decide if the thought you hold is worthwhile to keep around or if it should be replaced with something else.

Can I provide proof that my thought is valid or true with substantial, tangible evidence?

Can I think of an argument to disprove my thought?

Does this thought involve me making assumptions or jumping to conclusions I cannot possibly know is true?

How would my friend feel about this thought or situation? Would s/he disagree with it?

Does my situation or reaction change if I shift my focus from negative to positive? How would taking a positive outlook change my situation?

Will my circumstances or situation that are causing my anxiety or negative thoughts still be relevant in a month? A year? Five years from now?

Considering all of the above information, is this thought worth keeping? Is it beneficial?

How can I begin to replace this thought with something positive and productive?

Step 6 Activity 3: Outnumbering Negative Thoughts

Write down three negative thoughts you had today. For each one, write down three more positive thoughts about the subject of negative thought. Practice this within your day-to-day life as well this week. Every time you have one negative thought, you must follow it up with three positive thoughts, feelings, or observations about whatever triggered the negative thought.

Example:
Negative Thought: I am a bad person.
Positive thoughts:
- I care deeply about my friends.
- I try my hardest
- I would do anything to help my family.

Negative Thought:
Positive thoughts:
-
-
-

Negative Thought:
Positive thoughts:
-
-
-

Negative Thought:
Positive thoughts:
-
-
-

After a week of completing this exercise in real time, how do you feel? Did you notice any changes?.

STEP 7: REAL LIFE UTILIZATION

Congratulations! You have made it to the last step. Now, you are tasked with going out into the real world and maintaining the skills you have been developing up until this point. This is essentially you graduating from therapy. At this point, you are free to move on to other books to try to really solidify your skills, return to the beginning of this book to try to continue managing your anxiety or to go off on your own and attempt to manage your anxiety with the tools you have been given. At this point, you have the most important tools for managing your anxiety on your own.

When you go out into the real world with these skills, you will discover that you are better equipped to handling your ever-changing emotions. You will have the skills to keep yourself grounded, or at the very least, to give yourself the compassion you deserve when your anxiety symptoms do spring up again, and they will come back sometimes. Ultimately, this therapy seeks to give you the skills to manage your symptoms, so you no longer feel distressed by them, but it will never completely annihilate any feelings of anxiety. You will instead be able to recognize your anxiety as irrational and continue on with your life with that notion in mind. By disregarding your anxiety as irrational, you will feel better able to cope with the skills and not fall into the dangerous thinking traps of cognitive distortions or negative thoughts.

Try to use these skills at every opportunity that arises, as they give you control. With mindfulness, you can control your reactions to situations you have previously found troubling. Through identifying core beliefs, you will be able to identify the ways you think about yourself that are coloring your behaviors elsewhere in destructive ways. By identifying your negative thinking or cognitive distortions, you will be able to correct those as well, or at least recognize where you are likely to fall short in interacting with others. You need to recognize your weaknesses to really begin to develop your strengths, and CBT teaches you to identify your shortcomings.

Go into life knowing that CBT will not fix all of your problems, but it will teach you how to fix them. You will absolutely still feel your symptoms of anxiety sometimes. Your negative thoughts will crop up now and again and need to be re-challenged for you to regain control over them. Remember that these habits that you are trying to break are deeply ingrained in your mind and behaviors, and those behaviors will not disappear easily.

When you feel an anxiety attack coming on, use your grounding techniques and affirmations. These will help you to keep your anxiety under control. When you are able to achieve a state of mindfulness, always question your negative thoughts in order to try to challenge them so you can disregard them altogether. Remember the activities that taught you how to question your thoughts and go through the process of asking yourself if you can disprove them. When they are disproven, go through the effort of replacing your negative thought with a positive thought at the moment. Remember that an effective method of doing this is using your activity in outnumbering your negative thoughts.

Every time you have a negative thought, make it a point to replace it with something positive, or at the very least, drown it out with other positive points. Your mind will slowly adapt to using positivity when observing the world around you, and your behaviors will change to reflect this.

Now that you have a general idea of what to expect, let's consider an example. Imagine that you have social anxiety. Your friend wants you to go out to a special dinner to celebrate her promotion she has been working toward for ages at work, and after dinner, she wants you two to go out to a club for a few drinks. You happily agree, wanting to support your friend and show how happy you are for her, even though you know that you hate going out to events and social settings like those.

As the date creeps closer, you feel your anxiety coming up. Before, you would usually allow your anxiety to tell you that something bad must be coming simply by virtue of feeling anxious, but you remind yourself that

that is a cognitive distortion, and you cannot use emotional reasoning to dissuade yourself from going out and support your friend. You take a few deep breaths and remind yourself of your affirmation: "I am in control of my anxiety, and even though I may feel as though I am in danger, I recognize that it is my anxiety trying to fool me." Repeating that to yourself a few times, you feel your heart rate steady, and you continue about your day.

Despite telling yourself to pay your anxiety no mind, you feel a little more tense than normal as you go about your day. At work, one of your coworkers' pokes fun at a tiny mistake you made, not meaning to insult you but to playfully tease you for a quick laugh from the two of you. Usually, you would play along, but you immediately feel your blood pressure spikes, and your anxiety starts going crazy. You can feel a strong reaction to your coworker coming, and immediately, you try to focus on your grounding techniques to steady yourself. You go through identifying things around you with your various senses, and by the time you get to the third step in the sequence, you already feel yourself calming down. You quickly ask yourself what is upsetting you, and you realize that the answer is that your coworker teased you, and as you recently learned through your activities in this book, you have an inferiority complex, and the idea of making mistakes is a huge trigger for you. Immediately, you had felt attacked and vulnerable upon hearing your coworker teasing you.

By recognizing this, you are able to appeal to the rational side of your brain, reminding yourself that it had been a joke that was not meant to offend, and you repeat yet another affirmation. "I am capable, and I am worthy of the same compassion and understanding as everyone else. Everyone makes mistakes, and that is okay." Your anxiety attack is defused before it was ever able to explode in your face, and you are feeling pretty good about yourself, as so far, you have managed to cope with your anxiety, even when it threatened to overwhelm you.

Usually, by this point in the day, you would have given in to your anxiety and felt so worked up that you would have canceled your date with your friend. Instead, using your coping skills as necessary, you have been able to manage your anxiety. Things are looking up for you, and you head home from work to get ready to meet your friend for the night.

You go home and pull out your favorite outfit for a nice night on the town. You put in on, and as you do, you realize that the top is a bit tighter than normal, and immediately put yourself down, telling yourself that you should not be eating so much, or at the very least, you should be exercising more to keep your weight in check. After telling yourself this, you realize that you had a negative thought about yourself, insulting yourself for gaining weight. Taking a deep breath, you remind yourself of three things about your appearance that you do like in order to drown out the one negative thing you said.

Feeling pretty good overall at this point, you head out to meet your friend at the restaurant. You get in, and the two of you are settled in. You find that you and your friend are at a center table in the room, and again, you feel the familiar tendrils of anxiety reaching around your mind. You *hate* the inner table because of your anxiety, and it always makes you feel as though everyone is staring at you from all sides. Again, you return to your grounding techniques and take a few deep breaths. With a quiet reminder to yourself to calm down, you are able to continue throughout the night. You repeat another affirmation you use when you are feeling as though you are being watched or judged. "I am secure with who I am, and people around me likely are too busy paying attention to what they are doing to notice me."

Again, you appeal to the rational part of your mind, and you feel your anxiety flare starting to fade away. You are able to enjoy your dinner with your friend with only a few more deep breaths and affirmations when you felt your anxiety threatening to boil over again.

By the end of dinner, you are still feeling pretty in control of your emotions, although the anxiety is there, and you are aware of it. It becomes a minor annoyance that you are eventually able to tune out. You and your friend go to the club, and that is where you know your anxiety will really be tested.

The crowd, the loud noises, and the enclosed space surrounded by strangers are immediate triggers for you, and again, you must struggle to wrestle with your anxiety to remind yourself that you are in control and safe. Despite the anxiety screaming at you that something bad is going to happen, you remind yourself that your anxiety is attempting to predict the future, or a worst-case scenario and the likelihood of something bad happening there while you are enjoying your friend is slim to none. At worst, one of you might spill a drink or something.

Once again keeping your anxiety at bay, you are able to enjoy your night.

The entire night was enjoyed, and while you had some close calls that definitely would have stopped you from enjoying your day before, thanks to the CBT process, you were able to keep your anxiety under control. Your friend genuinely thanks you for the experience and tells you how proud she is that you managed to get through the whole night when crowds and public events are so difficult for you.

At that moment, you feel your first major victory: You were able to get through the entire day without letting anxiety control you. Your anxiety did not cause you to back out from your time with your friend, nor did cause you to blow up at your coworker. Through the steps provided in the book and with a better understanding of how your own mind works, you were able to avoid any major mishaps engaging in one of your biggest triggers.

No matter what your scenario is, or how it plays out, remember to use your skills in real time. Celebrate every success, no matter how small, and remember to treat yourself compassionately if you make mistakes. You are deserving of that compassion and understanding. This is not an easy process, nor is it a smooth one. You are bound to have slip-ups or mistakes, and that does not mean you are failing the process.

Before you go out on your own, here are three more skills to add to your arsenal and take with you as you attempt to navigate your triggers in real time.

Step 7 Activity 1: Grounding Yourself

People who suffer from panic attacks are all too familiar with the idea of being emotionally triggered. You may feel all of your anxiety symptoms on overdrive as your body reacts as though it is in grave danger. When this happens, having grounding techniques is essential to begin to engage your rational part of your brain. Only when you have returned your voice to your rational side of your brain will you be able to interrupt the panic attack in real time.

The next time you feel your panic or anxiety threatening to overwhelm yourself, try these simple grounding techniques.

1. Distractions: When you are feeling all of your worry and anxiety take over your mind, try to distract yourself so you can get control of the situation and address the source of the anxiety. Choose a color and look around your surroundings. Identify as many things as you can that have that color. Count them out as you do so. After you have found everything in color you have chosen, if you still feel stressed, you can choose another color and start over again.

2. Visualization: When in panic mode, sometimes your thoughts and feelings come in rapid sequence, so quickly that you feel overwhelmed. Take a moment to imagine each of your thoughts as fish in a river, or leaves on a tree that is falling off one by one as they pass. Instead of being overwhelmed by them all threaten to bury you, let them pass you by as quickly as they enter your mind. As soon as you feel a little more in control, you can identify why you are feeling the way you do and begin to address the root cause.

3. Rooting Yourself: This technique asks you to focus on your body. Scan your body from the top of your head and work your way down to your feet, focusing on each part slowly and deliberately. As you do this, imagine all of your tension following you down. Eventually, you will reach your feet, and you can imagine your tension and negative energy leaving your feet and entering the ground. You can imagine this as warmth, or assigning it a color, or anything else that works for you. Pay special attention to how you feel as the tension is released.

Now that you have grounded yourself with one of the above methods, or one that you create yourself using a similar structure, you should have entered a state of mindfulness that will allow you to rationally guide yourself out of the throes of anxiety and back to stable ground.

Step 7 Activity 2: Creating an Action Plan

Just as schools go through fire drills so the students are prepared if there ever is an actual fire because you will always respond better to an emergency when you have a rehearsed plan, you should create your own sort of plans to help you out of an emotional emergency. Choose a trigger for yourself and create a plan to help you handle it the next time you face it. Make sure this plan is specific and as detailed as possible in order to enable you to react in an effective manner.

Example:

Trigger: *Feeling criticized*

How you reacted last time: *I shut down emotionally and really struggled to get through my work because I have a fear of failure.*

How you will react differently next time: *I could remind myself that it is okay to make mistakes, and even though I did make a mistake, I am still a person worthy of respect.*

What do you think the results will be for your different reaction? *I will not get into as many fights because I will not take criticisms so personally.*

Trigger:

How you reacted last time:

How you will react differently next time:

What do you think the results will be for your different reactions?

Step 7 Activity 3: Real-Time Affirmations

Your affirmations are an effective skill, not only in the proper restructuring of your thoughts but also to use as a grounding tool when you feel your emotions starting to get the best of you. When tensions start to rise, or you feel as though you may be triggered, reciting your affirmations can be used to prompt you to make corrections in your behavior and keep the situation under control. This activity has you plan out three different affirmations you could use in a triggering situation.

Example:

Trigger: *Feeling abandoned or unloved*

Affirmation to ground yourself: *I am worthy of love and attention.*

Describe a situation that would use this: *If a friend has to cancel meeting up for something I was really looking forward to and I start to feel as though my friend does not really want to be my friend.*

Desired effect: *I will remind myself that my friend does, in fact, like to spend time with me, as he has reiterated on more than one occasion. Even though I may feel as though I am unlovable, I will remind myself that I am worthy of love and that reminder will be enough to keep my anxiety attack at bay.*

Trigger:
Affirmation to ground yourself:
Describe a situation that would use this:

Trigger:
Affirmation to ground yourself:
Describe a situation that would use this:

Trigger:
Affirmation to ground yourself:
Describe a situation that would use this:

CONCLUSION

Congratulations! You have made it to the end of this book. That is no small feat, especially if you were completing all of the steps and activities as you went along. This book crammed a lot into a short period in an effort to be as efficient and helpful as possible without being long-winded. Within these pages, you have discovered all of the key facets of completing cognitive behavioral therapy on your own without the need to seek a counselor.

During the course of reading this book, you were provided with the most important information to understanding what anxiety entails. You were provided with symptoms and common disorders, as well as a multitude of ways that anxiety can impact your life. From there, you were given all of the background information on cognitive behavioral therapy that you would need to complete the rest of this book successfully.

You were guided, step by step, through a process of cognitive restructuring. You began by learning how to identify thoughts that would need extra attention. You were also taught how to identify your emotional triggers. With all of the background information you needed on how to identify areas of your mind that needed restructuring, you were given the tools to begin challenging your negative thoughts, cognitive distortions, and your triggers. You were also given ways to begin the cognitive restructuring process, which allowed you to begin inserting positive thoughts in to replace the negative. Lastly, you were given some last-minute skills that would aid you in real life when you try to implement all of the changes on your own.

...ay, between the activities that this book provided you, and the ...yet comprehensive information you were given, you will begin to ...noticeable improvement in your symptoms of anxiety or frequency of . anxiety attacks. Remember that this is a long, arduous journey, and it ...ill take plenty of time, effort, and of course, missteps before you achieve the results you want. If it were easy to restructure your thoughts and banish anxiety, you would not be reading this book right now.

One last time, because this is so important to reiterate, if you feel as though your anxiety is unmanageable, even with the tools this book has provided you, please seek the advice of a medical professional. This book is not a substitute for medical advice or a medical professional and is meant to be a reference for yourself as opposed to a cure-all for anxiety. Remember that every person is different and has different needs, and if this book is not meeting the needs you have, there is no shame in moving on to another book, approach, or choosing to seek the guidance of a therapist to help you through this tough time. No matter how you choose to do it, know that you have the strength within you to alleviate your symptoms. You can, and will, manage your anxiety.

As you go off on your journey toward mental wellness, try to remember the key components this book advised. Seek to use your affirmations regularly, set SMART goals, and remember how to ground yourself when you are feeling emotionally volatile. Remind yourself that you can do this, and even when you feel like it is impossible, remind yourself that you *are* capable of doing it. You will just need to find the right toolset that works for you. Good luck on your journey to managing your anxiety, and I sincerely hope this book will be a valuable resource in that journey.

RECOMMENDED READINGS

Barlow, D. H., Craske, M. G. (2000). *Mastery of your anxiety and panic* (3rd Edition). San Antonio, TX: The Psychological Corporation.

Barlow, D.H. (2002). *Anxiety and Its Disorders: The Nature and Treatment of Anxiety and Panic* (2nd Edition). London: Guilford Press

Burns, D.D. (1980). *Feeling Good: The New Mood Therapy.* New York: Signet

Clark D.A., Beck A.T. (2010). *Cognitive Therapy of Anxiety Disorders* The Guilford Press, New York London

Clark D.M. (1986). A cognitive approach to panic. Behav. Res. Ther. 24, No. 4. pp. 461-470.

Craske M. G., Barlow D. H. (2008). *Panic Disorder and Agoraphobia.* In Clinical Handbook of Psychological Disorders, Fourth Edition: A Step-by-Step Treatment Manual.

Craske, M.G., Barlow, D.H. (2001). *Panic disorder and agoraphobia.* In D.H. Barlow (Ed.), Clinical Handbook Of Psychological Disorders, Third Edition. New York: Guilford Press.

Farmer R.E., Chapman A.L. (2008). *Behavioral Interventions in Cognitive*

herapy. Practical guidance for putting theory into action. American
.ogical Association, Washington

Fentz H.N., Hoffart A., Jensen M.B., Arendt M., O'Toole M.S., Rosen-
.erg N.K., Hougaard E. (2013). *Mechanisms of change in cognitive behaviour
therapy for panic disorder: The role of panic self-efficacy and catastrophic
misinterpretations.* Behaviour Research and Therapy 5, 579 e 587.

Freedman S., Adessky R. (2009). *Cognitive Behavior Therapy for Panic
Disorder.* Isr J Psychiatry Relat Sci, 46 No.4 251–256.

Nathan, P.R., Rees, C.S., Lim, L., & Smith, L.M. (2001). *Mood
Management – Anxiety: A Cognitive Behavioural Treatment Programme for Individual
Therapy.* Perth: Rioby Publishing.

Teachman B.A., Marker C.D., and Clerkin E. M. (2010). *Catastrophic
misinterpretations as a predictor of symptom change during treatment for panic disorder.*
J. Consult, Clin. Psychol. December; 78(6): 964–973.

White, K.S. Barlow, D.H. (2002). *Panic Disorder and Agoraphobia.* In D.H.
Barlow (Ed.), Anxiety and Its Disorders. Second Edition. New York:
Guilford Press.

ABOUT THE AUTHOR

Antonio Matteo Bruscella is a licensed psychologist who specialized in cognitive-behavioral treatments for anxiety, depression, insomnia, and other conditions. Dr. Bruscella is Chairman and founding member of the Lucana Association of Psychology and Cognitive Behavioural Therapy (ALPTCC) and member of the British Psychological Society (BPS)